THE AA EFFECT & WHY YOU'VE NEVER HEARD OF THE FDA-APPROVED DRUGS THAT TREAT ALCOHOLISM

Book 1

From the

RETHINKING DRINKING

Book Series

LINDA BURLISON

ADDICTION PUBLISHING

FIRST EDITION, VERSION 1.01

ISBN 978-0-9971076-8-5 Electronic Book Text
ISBN 978-0-9971076-9-2 Paperback

The AA Effect & Why You've Never Heard of the FDA-Approved Drugs that Treat Alcoholism / by Linda Burlison. – 1st Edition

Addiction Publishing, New York, N.Y.

Ordering
Special discounts are available on quantity purchases. For details, contact the publisher. Orders by trade bookstores and wholesalers welcome.

Publisher
Addiction Publishing
http://www.AddictionPublishing.com
linda@aprescriptionforalcoholics.com

Book Website
http://www.APrescriptionForAlcoholics.com

WHAT THE EXPERTS SAID

"It is highly disturbing that this drug is not made available to the patients that need it."[1]

–Report in Pharmacology & Therapeutics, 2006

•••

"There is an enormous gap between the number of alcohol use disorder patients [alcoholics] who would potentially benefit from medications and the number of patients who actually receive medications ... a recent study ... showed that nationally, only 3% of Veterans Health Administration patients with alcohol use disorder received treatment medications."[2]

–Report in American Journal of Psychiatry, 2014

•••

"There is no other comparable example in medicine where you *have* evidence-based treatments that are *not available*."[3]

–Dr. Shelly Greenfield, MD, Chief Academic Officer, McLean Hospital; Professor of Psychiatry, Harvard Medical School, 2012

•••

"People with addictive disorders continue to be offered, with great certitude and frequently at great cost, 'treatments' that are unsubstantiated by data or already known to be without beneficial effects...Meanwhile, advances that may be modest but have solid scientific support are arrogantly rejected by treatment providers in ways that would cause an uproar in other areas of medicine."[4]

–Dr. Markus Heilig, M.D., Ph.D., Former Chief of the Laboratory of Clinical Studies, and a Clinical Director at the US Institute of Alcohol Abuse, 2015

•••

"No experimental studies unequivocally demonstrated the effectiveness of AA or [12-step] approaches for reducing alcohol dependence... People considering attending AA or TSF [Twelve Step] programs should be made aware that there is a lack of experimental evidence on the effectiveness of such programs."[5]

–2006 Cochrane Review (Cochrane is one of the most credible and trusted scientific/medical review organizations in the world)

•••

"I'm not trying to eliminate AA...I'm just saying it should be prescribed to that tiny group who can make use of it... It's terribly harmful when you send 90 percent of the people for the wrong treatment advice."[6]

–Toronto Star article quoting Dr. Lance Dodes, Retired Professor of Psychiatry, Harvard Medical School, 2014

•••

"Medication-assisted treatment has shown much promise in reducing alcohol use and promoting abstinence in patients diagnosed with alcohol use disorder. Considerable research evidence and consensus among experts support the use of pharmacologic treatments...

A number of FDA-approved medications have been shown to be important elements of such treatment.

Although some patients do not benefit from medication-assisted treatment, most do. For each patient deemed an appropriate candidate for medication-assisted treatment, multiple pharmacologic agents offer a variety of options so that treatment can be tailored to each patient's needs and circumstances."[7]

–Free Guide from the Center for Substance Abuse Treatment, Substance Abuse and Mental Health Services Administration, US Department of Health and Human Services, 2013

IMPORTANT LEGAL NOTICES

Affiliations & Endorsements

The publisher and author are not affiliated with, do not endorse, nor recommend any products, brands, brand names, medications, substances, trademarks, companies, individuals, institutions, journals, doctors, writers, scientists, authors, personnel, or any industry (collectively, 'Third Parties') mentioned herein.

Third Parties mentioned herein belong to their respective owners, and are used without permission. Their use and any reference to, comment on, or mention of a Third Party is not intended to imply any endorsement of or direct (or indirect) affiliation with the Third Party.

Views expressed are solely the author's own. No Third Party has authorized, sponsored, or endorsed the content herein.

Risk

The reader ('you') expressly acknowledge and agree that neither the author nor the publisher nor its corporation ('we') are responsible for the results of your decisions resulting from the use of the Book, '*A Prescription for Alcoholics–Medications for Alcoholism*' ('the Book') or associated materials including forums or associated websites ('Related Materials'). Collectively, the Book and Related Materials shall be referred to as 'the content'.

Your use of the content acknowledges acceptance of these restrictions, disclaimers, and limitations. Use of the content is at your own risk.

We make no claim as to the accuracy of this information. You acknowledge that we have no control of or responsibility for your use of the content; have no knowledge of the specific or unique circumstances under which the content may be used by you; undertake no obligation to supplement or update the content of the book or related materials.

You assume all risk for selection and use of the content provided and for ensuring the appropriateness of using and relying upon the information in view of attendant circumstances, indications, and contraindications.

No Representation or Warranty

Except for warranties which may not be disclaimed as a matter of law, we make no representation or warranties whatsoever, express or implied, including but not limited to: representations or warranties regarding the accuracy or nature of the content; warranties of title; noninfringement; merchantability or fitness for a particular purpose; completeness; accuracy; reliability; completeness, suitability or availability with respect to the content of this book. We do not warrant that the information is true, current or non-misleading.

Every effort has been made to ensure that all information is accurate and complete, but no guarantee is made to that effect. We shall not be responsible for any errors, misstatements, inaccuracies or omissions regarding content. The content does not endorse any drug, pharmacy, diagnose patients, or recommend treatment.

References are provided for informational purposes only and do not constitute an endorsement of any websites or other sources. The websites listed may change. We are not medical or healthcare professionals.

ACKNOWLEDGMENTS

Thank-you Naomi for being such a beautiful, amazing, loving person.
I love you and am so proud of you, today and forever.

DEDICATION

In loving memory of Randy.

TABLE OF CONTENTS

PREFACE

WHERE TO START

In February of 2016 I published my first book, which was called *A Prescription for Alcoholics–Medications for Alcoholism*, and which I refer to here as the 'original book.'

It was the first book ever published to extensively cover an entire category of medications–FDA-approved medications–that have been proven effective in the treatment of alcoholism.

It also provided information about how to access the medication and get treatment, as well as providing detailed medical information about how alcoholism works in the brain.

I'm lucky enough to be able to say that I have never struggled with an addiction myself. Instead, my research was inspired by my friend Randy's battle with alcoholism.

The book you are reading now is part of the 4-book series that has emerged from the content of that original book.

Much of the content here was initially published in Part 1 of the original book. But it was a very long book, spanning over 550 pages, and covering a lot of topics! Perhaps there was too much information for many readers to wade through.

But now, by dividing the original book into four volumes, I hope to make the extensive information I collected even more accessible to anyone that needs it.

The primary goal of the original book was to let people know about the valid, well-researched pharmaceutical treatments that can help someone with alcoholism reduce or quit drinking.

Despite the enormous amount of scientific evidence supporting its effectiveness, as well as its endorsement at the most senior levels of US government, Medication Assisted Treatment (MAT) of alcoholism is rarely offered to alcoholics.

I also wanted to tell readers *why* it was that they may never have heard of MAT. I did this by highlighting the role of key players in alcoholism culture—Alcoholics Anonymous (AA), the medical community, the pharmaceutical industry and government. And finally I wanted to highlight some of the work done by crusaders in this area—people who have risked a great deal to educate others about medication that can treat alcoholism.

Here is short summary of what each book in the *Rethinking Drinking* series covers:

Book 1: The AA Effect & Why You've Never Heard of the FDA-Approved Drugs that Treat Alcoholism

Start here if you'd like to know about the quiet epidemic of deaths from untreated alcoholism, as well as why you may never before have heard of the numerous medications that can help people with alcohol dependence reduce and/or quit drinking.

It covers the role of key players in alcoholism culture, as well as the journey through where we've been, where we are, and what we need to do next.

Book 2: Understanding Alcoholism as a Brain Disease

Start here if you'd like a better understanding of the brain disease called alcoholism.

This book includes an in-depth explanation of how alcoholism works inside the brain; the stages of alcoholism identified by researchers; and a list of clues to your genetic vulnerability.

If you haven't thought about alcoholism from a true medical perspective before, this book may be of help to you. Written in plain English, even if you aren't a doctor or scientist, you'll find this book easy to read and understand.

Book 3: Reduce or Stop Drinking with Medication – The How-To Guide

If you are considering taking medication to treat alcoholism, but are wondering where to begin, start with this book–Book 3.

You'll learn everything you need to know to obtain treatment with medication including finding a doctor and obtaining medication.

This book includes information on determining goals, tracking results, developing a medication strategy, combining medications, determining what type of alcoholism you may have, how to obtain medication, and many other considerations.

Book 4: Medications to Reduce or Quit Drinking – The Drug Compendium

Start here if you would like in-depth information about specific medications and the research that backs them up.

This book contains invaluable research, insights and links to additional resources that will help you and your doctor to determine which medications are right for you. There is also an important section covering drugs (some of them very common), which may cause some people to actually increase their drinking.

Here you'll find over 200 pages of detailed, meticulously researched information on drugs that can treat alcoholism.

Highlights from over 300 scientific research reports are referenced and summarized.

This book is divided into four lists:

1) The A-List–Most Important Medications Today

2) The B-List–Medications Worth Consideration Today

3) The D-List–Eleven Drugs that May Increase Drinking

4) The Futures List–Sixty+ Drugs to Watch

I encourage you to photocopy sections of Book 4 to bring to your doctor, and also visit the book's website (APrescriptionForAlcoholics.com) to access and print the most important research highlighted for each medication.

SPREAD THE WORD

If this book has made a difference to you, please consider helping to spread the word.

You can do this by:

- Sharing a free chapter found on the website with a friend (www.APrescriptionforAlcoholics.com)

- Passing the book on to someone you know.

- Donating a few copies to a library, school, doctor's office or recovery program.

Posting about the book on social media.

CHAPTER ONE

01 | INTRODUCTION

*"When a well-packaged web of lies has been sold gradually
to the masses over generations, the truth will seem utterly
preposterous and its speaker a raving lunatic."*

–Donald James Wheal

PUZZLE PIECES

My friend Randy was an alcoholic. And like many people who care about someone with this devastating disease, I looked high and low for solutions for his alcoholism.

It's just what we do.

Alcoholism was a cage Randy lived his life in, and I wanted to help him escape so he could live the life he was meant to live.

As I was searching for a solution, I came across research about medications that were showing promise in helping alcoholics.

And I came across many stories—very credible-sounding stories—of people for whom medication was working.

Over months, I put together a picture of this world. It was like a jigsaw puzzle—one research article here talking about one medication, another article there about a different medication. A disappointing dead-end here, a hopeful new pathway there.

I learned a new language so that I could understand what I was reading—'neuroplasticity', 'allele,' 'homeostasis,' 'neuroadaptation'…no wonder we don't understand alcoholism very well—it comes with its own vocabulary.

I also learned alcoholism is responsible for more deaths worldwide each year than any other illness.[89]

And I learned the little-known fact that there are numerous FDA-approved medications available that are as effective and safe in alcoholism as common anti-depressants are in fighting depression.

But the medical profession hasn't paid attention to this research.

So the tiny percentage of people who actually receive treatment (around eight percent[10]), are shepherded into 12-step program-based treatments which reinforce dangerous misperceptions about the disease and have a dismal 90-95% failure rate[6] and no scientific evidence of effectiveness.[5]

'Write the book you want to read,' is a phrase I recently came across. So I did.

It's true that you can only help an alcoholic who wishes to be helped. But if you know one, or you are one, at least you can find all of this information in one place now.

In this book series, I've pulled together all of the research on all of the medications that have been shown to help alcoholics, so that you don't have to.

Along the Way

Along the way in my own journey with the alcoholic in my life I saw tragic gaps in our system.

I realized that my own beliefs about alcoholism were outdated and misinformed. I came to see that outdated beliefs reinforce the system we have in place right now—which doesn't work.

I hope you'll question your own beliefs as you read this book because some commonly-held beliefs about alcohol addiction are helping to kill a lot of people.

I also hope that the book will contribute to an informed conversation about how we can stop treating alcoholism like a shameful personality disorder and start treating it like the neurobiological disease that it is.

There is too much needless suffering for alcoholics and their loved ones. It's time to put an end to that.

This Book is Based on Research

Please put aside any assumptions you may have that just because you may not have heard about the medications this book refers to that they do not work.

Thousands of lives (but just a tiny number in comparison to those they could have helped) have been saved because of the drugs referenced in this book.

It is tragic, though, how many alcoholics still die without ever learning that medication was even an option.

There is *solid medical research* supporting the safety and effectiveness of many of the drugs I discuss.

And when I write the phrase 'solid medical research,' I'm not referring to the kind of thing you hear on a late night infomercial or one random study done in 1975 pulled out of a third rate archive somewhere.

I'm referring to hundreds of studies completed by the top research and medical bodies in the world, conducted and written about by the top addiction researchers in the world and published in the top medical journals.

I wrote this book series using the life work of over 2000 scientists. I have collected and read over 700 of the studies written by these individuals and have provided summaries of key findings for many of them in volume 4 of this series ('Medications to Reduce or Quit Drinking – the Drug Compendium.')

A sampling of sources of these studies include:

- The three bodies responsible for regulating and determining which medications can be prescribed in North America and Europe: American FDA, Health Canada, Europe's EMA (European Medicines Agency);

- The US National Library of Medicine (www.nlm.nih.gov and livertox.nih.gov);

- Work published in journals such as the European Pharmaceutical Review, the British Journal of Medicine and Medical Research, the Journal of Clinical Psychopharmacology, the American Journal of Psychiatry, the New England Journal of Medicine, The Journal of Addiction Medicine, JAMA, the

Cochrane Database of Systematic Reviews, The American Journal of Drug and Alcohol Abuse, The International Journal of Neuropsychopharmacology, Pharmacology Biochemistry and Behavior, and many others.

- Research conducted by the top addiction scientists and doctors in the world. People like Giovanni Addolorato, Bankole A. Johnson, George F. Koob, Markus Heilig, Barbara J. Mason, David Nutt, Rainer Spanagel, Robert M. Swift, Wim van den Brink, Raymond F. Anton, Lara A. Ray, Albert J. Arias, Renaud De Beaurepaire, Jonathan Chick, Ciraulo A. Domenic, James C Garbutt, Antoni Gual, George A. Kenna, Henry R. Kranzler, Lorenzo Leggio, Karl Mann, Helen M. Pettinati, David Sinclair and hundreds of others.

- Research endorsed by the top addiction medicine institutions and organizations in the world such as the National Institute on Alcohol Abuse and Alcoholism (NIAAA), National Institute on Drug Abuse (NIDA), The Scripps Research Institute (TSRI), the Canadian Association for Addiction and Mental Health (CAMH), American Psychiatric Association (APA), the American College of Neuropsychopharmacology (ACNP) and many others.

THIS IS FOR YOU

WHO CAN THIS BOOK SERIES HELP?

It has been pointed out to me that there are many people who do not define themselves as alcoholic, but instead see themselves as a 'heavy drinker' or a 'binge drinker', or define their drinking using another term altogether.

Some people notice that they are beginning to think about alcohol a great deal, or are starting to notice a disturbing pattern in their consumption, but would not call themselves alcoholic.

While I researched and wrote this book with the severe alcoholic in mind, whether you are one, or are just someone who feels they may be heading in the wrong direction, the medications in this book may be able to help you.

I use the terms 'alcoholic,' 'alcoholism,' 'alcohol dependence,' and 'addiction' throughout the book.

Some people now prefer the term 'Alcohol Use Disorder', which is often just shortened to 'AUD'.

While 'AUD' may be the term adopted in the years ahead, I felt it was important to use terms that most people are familiar with.

Definitions are important. But ultimately, I'm most concerned about letting people who can benefit from medication know about them. If alcohol dependence is becoming a problem, or is already a problem, this book is for you.

As one addiction expert says, "If you can't live with it, and can't live without it, you're in trouble. That is the only definition of addiction that matters."[11]

DEAR ALCOHOLIC

If you are suffering from alcoholism, the last thing I want to do is give you false hope. There is no magic bullet for most people, and these medications don't work for everyone.

Many of them have side effects, but they are usually tolerable and have been shown to disappear after safe discontinuation.

The vast majority of them are completely non-addictive and are safely prescribed by doctors for other medical purposes.

If you are one of the few who have tried a medication before, this book series may shed light on why it did or did not work for you and can offer ideas about next steps or combinations to try.

The good news is that these medications can save lives. Maybe one of them will be yours.

So, if you are an alcoholic, I hope that you will ask yourself one question as you read this book:

What do I have to lose?

WHAT WE KNOW FOR SURE

It ain't what you don't know that gets you into trouble.

It's what you know for sure that just ain't so.

—Mark Twain/The Big Short

I know many people who believe strongly in AA (Alcoholics Anonymous). And I know many people who believe in people that believe strongly in AA. If you are one of those people, this section is for you.

Many of these individuals are the salt of the earth. They'd give the shirt off their backs if you needed it.

Is it possible, as this book proposes, that all these good people could be so wrong?

Unfortunately, yes.

It reminds me of the bird washers.

Have you ever heard the stories about people that go to oil spills, put their lives aside and spend day and night cleaning and caring for birds who are covered by oil from the spill?

The people who do this work are good-hearted people who just want to help. I thank goodness that there are people like that in the world because they make it a better place.

It was surprising to me to hear about studies the other day that show that more than 99% of the cleaned birds die anyway.[12]

After the traumatic capture and cleaning process, many of the birds die slowly and painfully, out of sight, a week or two later, from liver and kidney damage.

Now, imagine being one of those well-intended, caring people who spend many hope-filled hours cleaning distressed birds, and then hearing the news that instead of helping them to live, you were actually just torturing one bird at a time on its way to an inevitable demise.

I probably would *not* want to accept what I was told.

I would probably try to cast doubt on those studies and defend my own actions.

I would cite examples of birds I knew I had helped, who had lived out long, wonderfully spiritual lives after the cleaning.

Initially, I'd probably do anything to feel like what I had been doing was the right thing.

It's human nature: we don't want to realize we have done something wrong—especially when life and death are at stake, and when we have done that thing with all our heart and soul and best intentions.

That is an uncomfortable, even painful feeling.

Eventually, if I were a former bird-scrubber, with enough evidence, I would probably come to accept the truth.

If my ego could handle it, I might start to advocate for a different way to help the birds. I would know that my heart was always in the right place, but that my actions were simply guided by my best intentions and the information I had at the time.

•••

Alcoholism is polarizing.

When we are polarized, we close our minds.

Are you a health care professional, an AA member or someone who can't believe that medication could help an alcoholic? This book will certainly challenge your beliefs.

This book may tell you some things you don't want to hear, and which might make you feel uncomfortable. You may even feel angry at me right now.

But I'm just the bearer of information. I challenge you to put aside your skepticism for a few days. Stop listening to other bird scrubbers for a week; read the book, read the research, and then make your own conclusions.

As you read this book, if you are a skeptic, you may from time to time, need to think of yourself as that well-intentioned bird-scrubber, helping yourself or the alcoholics(s) in your life in the best way you could.

As you read, you might feel uncomfortable because you may begin to think that something you believed to be true–something you participated in–isn't so true, and while you had nothing but the best intentions, you might realize that there is a better way.

Instead of running from that uncomfortable feeling, I hope you can use it as rocket fuel for the good that you do next.

The goodness of our hearts can stay the same while what we do next can be very different.

WHAT THIS BOOK DOESN'T COVER

WITHDRAWAL MEDICATION

There are three categories of medication for alcoholics–those for withdrawal, those to deter drinking; and those that fight characteristics of the disease itself (extending abstinence, reducing cravings, reducing drink consumption).

Withdrawn medications need to be used more often. Alcohol Withdrawal Syndrome (AWS) can be fatal and should be treated medically. However, this book does not focus on them.

Drinking deterrents (like disulfiram) are useful for some, but dangerous for many others. A few are mentioned in the book.

This book focusses primarily on the third category: medication that fights the disease at its root–in the brain. These are medications that can slow or halt the progression of the disease itself.

TREATMENT OF CONCURRENT DISORDERS

Many individuals suffer from multiple concurrent disorders–for example, many alcoholics experience depression and anxiety, and a high percentage of people with schizophrenia are also addicted to alcohol.

Some researchers hypothesize that the cause of alcoholism for many individuals is a related mental illness that they have tried to medicate with alcohol. (And if you are one of these individuals who has been prescribed an SSRI, please know that there is research—detailed in Volume 4—that shows that some SSRI's and other common medications can actually *increase* drinking in some alcoholics.)

There is significant research now that looks at concurrent disorders, and while this research has not been excluded from the book, and in fact, some of the research highlighted touches on concurrent disorders, the primary focus of research and information in this book is for the treatment for alcoholism alone.

02 | SAD STORIES

"I'm sick of seeing people suffer needlessly and die needlessly.

The assumptions upon which the North American approach to addiction has been based since the early 20th century are mistaken, nasty, and stupid—when it comes right down to it, they amount to genocide."[13]

—Dr. Peter Ferentzy, Addiction Scientist

NOT A COMEDY ROUTINE

There is a popular talk-show on TV that sometimes features a character named Sue, who often appears on the show drinking from a bottle of wine.

She seems to be drinking large quantities of alcohol and making poor, sometimes dangerous decisions. Sue falls off of things, wobbles around on too-high heels and acts promiscuously and inappropriately. In one show, with a glass of wine in one hand she topples off a roof to her death.

It's all a lighthearted act, just to make us laugh, and part of me says that it's harmless. I wouldn't have thought twice about it a few years ago.

But another part of me looks at Sue and isn't laughing. I've heard too many sad stories about the real Sues out there.

We don't laugh at cancer or other painful diseases, so why do we laugh at alcoholism? Perhaps we don't connect the often clown-like behavior of the alcoholic to the realities of the disease.

Maybe we need to connect the dots.

CONNECTING THE DOTS

Alcohol dependence is chronic, severe mental disorder characterized by bouts of compulsive and uncontrolled drinking, and an inability to cut down drinking despite the knowledge of its harmful, sometimes fatal consequences.

Worldwide, the World Health Organization says 3.3 million deaths can be attributed to alcohol abuse or dependence each year.[9] They estimate that alcohol is the international number one killer, ahead of AIDS.[8]

Nearly 18 million Americans suffer from alcoholism[14] and the United States spends nearly $35 billion a year[15] on alcohol- and substance-abuse treatment.

And every year, 88,000[14] people in the United States die from this disease anyway.

That's more people than can fit into the Houston Astrodome.

And those are just the ones that die.

Alcoholism is a family disease–it devastates families–so imagine for every person in that Astrodome that has died, there are children, parents, siblings, spouses–people, whose families have been torn apart because one member of it just can't seem to stop lifting that bottle to their mouth.

And alcoholism isn't just a disease–it's a disease maker.

Two hundred different potentially fatal health conditions are brought on by alcoholism.

Alcohol is the root cause of 50% of deaths from liver cirrhosis, 30% of deaths from all oral and pharynx cancers, 25% of deaths from all pancreatitis, 23% of deaths from all laryngeal cancers, 22% of deaths from all oesophageal cancers, 22% of deaths from interpersonal violence, 22% of all deaths from self-harm, 14% of all deaths from poisoning, and on and on and on.[9]

In the UK, 80% of deaths from liver diseases are due to alcohol and while deaths from all other major diseases have seen a gradual decrease, there has been a relentless increase in liver disease related deaths in the last twenty years with mortality rates increasing a staggering five-fold.

Alcohol is the most common reason for death in men under 50 and 20% of all deaths in men aged 16-44 are due to alcohol.[16]

It's an epidemic that respected professor and former chief drug adviser to the government, Dr. David Nutt, called a "public health emergency."[17][18]

Nutt's 2010 research in the respected Lancet looked at 100 drugs and compared the harm they cause to the individual who uses them as well as that caused to those beyond the misuser.

Overall, alcohol was found to be significantly more harmful to the drinker and to others around them than even heroin and crack cocaine.

Its impact on others beyond the alcoholic is born out in statistics in areas such as child abuse and drunk driving fatalities.

In the United States, it's estimated that drunk driving costs $199 billion per year. In 2013, over 10,000 people died and 290,000 were injured in drunk driving crashes.

Alcoholism is a major factor in these accidents since despite the significant repercussions if convicted of drunk driving, one-third of all drivers arrested or convicted are repeat offenders, and the average drunk driver has driven drunk 80 times before their first arrest.[19]

Alcoholism rips families apart and results in isolation, loss of self-esteem, and physical, mental, financial suffering that is beyond measure.

The American Academy of Child & Adolescent Psychiatry estimates that one in five adult Americans have lived with an alcoholic relative while growing up and that most children of alcoholics have experienced neglect or abuse.[20]

And alcoholics have an extremely high risk of suicide—5,080 times that of the general population.[21]

Addiction isn't a comedy routine.

As French-American cardiologist and former alcoholic, the late Dr. Olivier Ameisen wrote:

"Addiction is a living nightmare in which you wake up *to* the horror, not *from* it."[22]

MY LIFE IN BEER MARKETING

Hi, I'm Linda and I'm a former beer marketer. But don't discount me yet.

It's not the tragic epidemic of alcoholism described in the last chapter that motivated me to write this book.

As with many people, I ignore most problems until they hit me in the face and become personal.

I'll tell you what made this personal soon, but first I can perhaps best explain my qualifications for writing this book by telling you what I am not.

I am not a doctor, who has bought into my community's dogma;

I'm not a scientist who has sought research funding from a pharmaceutical company or committed my life to a particular research direction, or a pharma executive trying to pitch the next profitable drug;

I'm not an AA member committed to the AA way; I don't make a living selling a counselling program, a herbal supplement or a meditative retreat. I'm not a part of the alcoholism research or medical or rehab community in any way.

I'm also not an alcoholic who needs to rely on the system for help or is afraid to 'out' myself at work or in my community.

I don't have to be careful about who I offend for fear that I won't be funded again, that an important organization will boycott my clinic; or the only friends I have in the world won't call me again.

My lack of qualification and sponsorship means that in some ways I am the ideal person to write this book, because as a friend pointed out to me, sometimes it takes someone who is completely and utterly outside the system to hold up a mirror to it.

I'm simple: I see a devastating problem with enormous magnitude. And I see solutions that aren't being used to fix this problem. And I think enough is enough.

•••

Ten years ago, before I knew anything about alcoholism, I worked for a great guy I'll call Mark, and we did alcohol marketing together.

For a time, we worked in the head office of one of the two major Canadian breweries, and under Mark's leadership built and managed all of their beer brand websites for them.

A few years later I worked (at an advertising agency this time) for the other major Canadian brewery, doing similar work. During these years, I was the first person in Canada (maybe North America) to create and run search engine marketing campaigns to promote beer brands, and the agency I worked at was the first to run social media campaigns for beer companies.

One of the things I learned back then was that our target group for much of that marketing was men who consumed 13+ drinks per day. (The only exception was the social media marketing, which aimed at a much younger demographic).

We spent half our time trying to figure out how to reach more of them. I sometimes wondered if that was ethical–weren't we targeting alcoholics?

More recently I came across the statistic that 15% of drinkers consume 75%[23] of all alcohol and the top 10% of drinkers average nearly 9 drinks a day[23]–so now I know we *were* targeting alcoholics. It was an inconvenient truth in the business of alcohol marketing then, as it is now.

Ten years later, as I started writing this book, I was once again working for Mark and found myself asking him for time off from work (we long ago stopped working on any alcohol marketing), so that I could write a book about alcoholism and its treatments.

By that time, I had a very close friend who was dying of alcoholism, and Mark's dad had already died from it.

Sad Stories

In an attempt to understand alcoholism and how to deal with it, I used to go to support groups for the families and friends of people with alcoholism. I attended quite a lot of AA meetings too with my friend Randy.

They were hopeful meetings full of kind people. But they offered no solutions.

One day, I began to research and learn about alcoholism. I read the medical and scientific research about it. And the more I learned, the harder it became for me to attend these meetings. It became more difficult to look at the faces of the people there.

There was a sweet elderly couple that could be your grandparents that cried about their daughter's addiction.

There was an angry suburban mother with two little boys whose sister was killed by a drunk driver when she was four and whose father and husband are both alcoholics. Alcoholism has a funny way of 'clustering'.

There was a lady–the wife of a wealthy doctor–whose daughter was in the hospital just after I started writing this book. The daughter was a beautiful girl. She was my age. Later I learned she had gone to the high school where some of my friends had gone, where she had starred in the school's musicals. Her mother–stressed and overwhelmed–could have been my mother–anyone's mother.

I remember the mom coming to a meeting in the winter in such distress one day that she wore mismatched boots on her feet. It was hard not to notice as we sat in a circle.

I put the daughter's obituary with her pretty face on the wall next to my desk many months ago as a reminder to keep on writing.

There were usually 20 people sitting in the room, all of whom had such sad stories. But they weren't at the meetings for solutions.

They were there to learn to follow the serenity prayer and 'accept the things they could not change.'

I found it very hard to keep attending because the most frustrating and tragic thing was that the more I learned, the more I knew it didn't have to be that way.

I'm not a 'bleeding heart' kind of a person.

But I cannot stand seeing the stupid, needless waste of human life, and the pain it leaves behind when it is sitting right next to me in the same circle.

These people and thousands of people like them were why I wrote this book.

IT'S PERSONAL

"If I can turn her death, and that of many others, into a victory of some kind, then maybe it'll all make sense.
Or, maybe it'll just seem a little less stupid."[11]

Randy was a severe alcoholic. And of course he was the reason I started attending those meetings and researching medications for alcoholism in the first place.

I wish, with all my heart that I could say that the medications in this book saved Randy and that he now lives the amazing life he was always meant to live.

Maybe in a parallel universe he has a beautiful wife, a house with a picket fence, a fast boat, and a dog named Kali.

But in this universe we don't see him anymore.

I sat down and began to write the book in February 2015. About 300 pages into its writing, my dear friend took his life.

He couldn't do it anymore. He didn't want to hurt his friends and family any longer. He couldn't live with it, and he couldn't stop drinking, so he stopped the only way he could.

Randy died, as his alcoholic father had and as too many alcoholics do, by his own hand, leaving a trail of pain, trouble, debt, legal and financial problems, heartache and loss behind him.

And in the strange repeating pattern which is alcoholism, Randy left a son behind too.

The sadness inside me at his loss is not something that words can describe. Guilt made me feel I should have done more.

I took a month off from the book, told his friends, organized his funeral, looked after his belongings, cried a lot of tears and started writing again.

His funeral, held in August 2015, was standing-room only. He called himself a monster, but he was, in fact, a special and rare individual and he was indeed loved as a fellow human being, not a monster. He was a man who, even in the weeks before he died, lit up a room with his good looks and smile, musical talents, and ability to charm those around him.

When Randy died, it occurred to me that it would not be very inspiring to read a book about medications for alcoholism where the 'main character' was not saved by the solution the book proffered.

But this book isn't about proof of efficacy from one person. Nor should it be—the whole point of drawing conclusions from scientific research is that it is repeatable and statistically significant.

So had he survived alcoholism, Randy's single successful data point would have been just as immaterial to this book as is his death.

There is too much medical research backing these medications—the data exists, and I don't mean it exists in the form of a few stray outliers. It is solid. Read it, and I challenge you to tell me it is not.

Randy was tormented by alcoholism and desperate for help. He was a committed AA member and tried to get real help for his alcoholism for 20+ years.

He ashamedly tucked his tail between his legs after numerous destructive binges and walked back through the doors of those rooms over and over again.

He also tried to get help from many non-AA organizations, attending programs at hospitals and treatment centers.

During this time, he was never once offered one of the medications in this book, unprompted, by any medical professional he ever saw.

And he saw dozens—doctors, psychiatrists, social works, occupational therapists, health care workers and all manner of addiction specialists—if not over a hundred of them as his illness progressed.

After facing many difficult and frankly ridiculous roadblocks in even obtaining them, Randy responded well to one of the medications discussed later. I believe strongly that had he received long-term Medication Assisted Treatment (MAT) many years ago before the disease progressed so far, he would have had a fighting chance.

By the time he died, however, he was a severe, long-term alcoholic.

And unfortunately, even after jumping through hoops to get treatment from the leading addiction treatment organization in our country, bringing with him pages of research, he could not find a doctor there willing to support him in prescribing the medications in ways shown to be effective. Instead, he was referred back to AA.

Had I held a crystal ball up for the last "addiction specialist" he saw, revealing that healthy-looking, sober, smiling Randy would be dead two months later after a protracted binge, would that doctor have taken the disease seriously enough to prescribe the medications and support that Randy asked for?

I'll never know and I guess it doesn't matter anymore, other than to fuel me to want to help other people get the help that Randy couldn't get.

I talked to him about this book. I wanted him to know that his life and experiences weren't a waste–they could help people we would never meet. He told me to tell his story.

I hope (as he did) that you can learn from him, and I hope his death will remind you of the deadly serious nature of alcoholism. This disease can kill you or your loved one too. It's no joke.

During my friendship with him, I saw how Randy was treated by the medical and healthcare community; how he was eventually shunned by members of his family; how many of his experiences in fighting a medical illness were so demeaning. Eventually the system just abandoned him. There was no solution for him that they could offer.

Randy's life was an example of a person being processed through a broken system and coming out dead on the other end.

So it's not just that I want medication, or better yet–Medication Assisted Treatment–to be available to people who need it. I want the whole system to be better. I want this book to help change the way we treat and look at alcoholics.

03 | YESTERDAY & TODAY

"A complex brain disease requires many approaches, the addiction field needs to bring the best of these together, not fight over who's right."

–Hazelton Doctor Marvin Seppala

HEADLINES

As new discoveries have emerged, so has evidence showing that alcoholism can be treated safely and effectively with medication–like any other illness.

But unfortunately, in the last twenty years, little of the scientific body of work supporting medication for alcohol addiction treatment has translated into readily available treatment options for those suffering from the disease.

There is a profound gap between what we know and the treatment people receive.

Good, FDA-approved medications to treat alcoholism have been available for many years, but until recently 'alcohol culture' wasn't ready for them.

But we are now at a tipping point.

If a tipping point could have a name, this one would be called Matt.

Or actually–MAT–which is short for "Medication Assisted Treatment'.

It's a new phrase that is emerging, used by clever spin-doctors in the US government, peppered into reports from the country's top health, drug and addiction organizations, and finding its way into newspaper articles and addiction websites.

The first surprising headlines of change started in 2012.

A long-time-stronghold of 12-step treatment–Hazelton–shocked the recovery community when it introduced anti-addiction medication into their recovery programs for the first time in history.

Time Magazine quoted Dr. Marvin Sepala, Hazelton's Chief Medical Officer saying, "This is a huge shift in our culture and organization... we believe it's the responsible thing to do."[24]

Shortly afterward, in Europe in 2013, pharmaceutical company Lundbeck made headlines when it launched the first drug approved in over a decade (nalmefene) for alcohol-dependent patients with high-risk drinking levels.[25]

Then in 2014, under a swell of pressure from advocates and alcoholics, French health authorities gave the green light to doctors to formally prescribe a drug called baclofen to treat people with an addiction to alcohol.[26]

Recently, in the US in February 2015, Obama's government made a historic appointment, which kicked off a tidal wave of change.

The Washington Post headline proclaimed: "Drug Czar Approaches Challenge from a Different Angle: As a Recovering Alcoholic." Instead of another militant leader to fight the war on drugs, the US brought in someone with his own criminal record.

Obama had appointed Michael Botticelli–a recovering alcoholic with a DUI on file.

Sober for over 26 years, and despite his strong ties to 'anti-medication' AA, Botticelli is fighting for evidence-based treatment (which means medication) for substance abuse treatment.[27]

The Drug Czar appointment was followed up quickly with two more government announcements in February and March.

The first was from The Substance Abuse and Mental Health Services Administration about the new use of penalties for judges that order addicts (including alcoholics) off of medically assisted treatment:

"Drug courts that receive federal dollars will no longer be allowed to ban the kinds of medication-assisted treatments that doctors and scientists view as the most effective care.... We've made that clear: If they want our federal dollars, they cannot do that."[28]

The second was an announcement that for the first time in the United States, the Affordable Care Act would legislate that substance abuse must be treated like any other illness:

"These rules are...a sea change in the way that health plans approach the coverage of mental health and substance abuse disorder benefits ... Essentially, President Obama's health care act enshrines in federal law that substance abuse is a medical issue—not the result of poor morals, and not a criminal justice problem."[28]

However, as we'll see later in this book, all the government legislation in the world makes no difference to the use of medication if pharmaceutical companies cannot be profitable in making it and doctors won't prescribe it.

But for the first time in North America in 2015, a medication that can be used for the treatment of opioid and alcohol dependence saw profitability.

In October 2015, Alkermes Pharmaceutical's historic press release announced that they were improving their financial expectations for the remainder of the year, driven by the accelerating growth in net sales of their naltrexone injection product Vivitrol, which had experienced an unprecedented sales increase of 72%.

Around the world, pharmaceutical company CEOs turned their heads and tipped their hats at Alkermes. It was a clear signal that a category of medication once avoided and practically hidden from shareholders could now be profitable.[29]

And finally, most recently, in October 2015, in front of President Obama, Botticelli, senators and a crowd of people in Charleston

West Virginia, Secretary of Health and Human Services, Sylvia Burwell spoke of their new priorities around substance abuse, saying:

> "Number one is changing prescribing practices... and second is working on medication assisted treatment."[30]

Finally... MAT might end up on your doctor's prescription pad.

Times they are a'changin. And not a moment too soon.

SO OVERDUE

These events are overdue–woefully overdue.

The state of treatment for people with alcoholism is shameful.

Nowhere in the field of modern medicine is treatment more antiquated than in the area of alcohol addiction treatment, where time has stood still since AA's Big Book was published in 1939.[15]

In the last 25 years, cancer death rates have gone down by 22% while in the same period addiction overdose death rates have tripled.[31]

A 2012, exceptionally well-written report from the National Center on Addiction and Substance Abuse (Entitled '*Addiction Medicine: Closing the Gap Between Science & Practice*') compared the current state of addiction medicine to general medicine in the early 1900s.

The report said: "The vast majority of people in need of addiction treatment do not receive anything that approximates evidence-based care."[3]

Markus Heilig, an internationally respected addiction researcher, and doctor, recently wrote:

"People with addictive disorders continue to be offered, with great certitude and frequently at great cost, "treatments" that are unsubstantiated by data or already known to be without beneficial effects.

Meanwhile, advances that may be modest but have solid scientific support are arrogantly rejected by treatment providers in ways that would cause an uproar in other areas of medicine."[4]

FDA-approved drugs exist which may be even more effective at battling alcoholism than widely prescribed drugs such as cholesterol-lowering statins are at fighting heart disease.[14]

Yet in the US, of the approximately 19 million patients meeting criteria for alcohol dependence, less than 150,000 are treated with FDA-approved pharmacotherapy.[32]

However, most shockingly, the medications proven most effective and life changing for alcoholics have been researched and FDA-approved for decades.

•••

I don't remember the day that I went to my computer and started the Googling that led me to the research that ultimately led to writing this book.

But I do know that the more I read, the more I wondered how it was possible that in the year 2015, an area of medicine for a major disease could be so backward.

And I also noticed that unlike most major illnesses, where government, pharmaceutical companies, not-for-profits and medical institutions play the leading roles in educating consumers about medical treatment, many of these stakeholders were strangely quiet when it came to this particular illness.

There was a curious void of information about medical treatment from the usual suspects.

In fact, there seemed to be only two groups of people who were sharing information about medical solutions: uber geeks and advocate alcoholics.

The uber geeks (okay–'scientific researchers') were slogging away in labs and at conferences, working hard despite growing frustration that their discoveries were not reaching the critical mass of people they should be helping.

And as good as they are at research and report writing, they seem in equal parts weak or uninterested in translating their work into plain English and making it accessible to alcoholics and their treatment providers.

On the other hand, the advocate alcoholics were a passionate, outspoken and interesting bunch.

For the small group of people who have been lucky enough to learn about these medications, it is the advocate alcoholics that are mostly to thank.

This group includes recovering doctors who walked away from careers, outing their own alcoholism to write about medication that saved their lives; public figures who abandoned anonymity in the face of heavy stigma to push for more public awareness, and hundreds of recovering alcoholics from all walks of life who reached out online (both anonymously and publicly) to help others discover and access these medications.

Most of the material written in plain English in book form and online that currently exists and is related to this area of medicine comes from this group.

Highlighting the void of information from the usual sources is this: one of the best (and only) documentaries on one of these medications–*One Little Pill*–comes not from any government organization or pharmaceutical company, but was crowd-funded and produced by one of these advocate alcoholics I speak of. This advocate also started an organization with branches in the US and Europe to help alcoholics access the medication that helped her.

I'm speaking of Claudia Christian here. She's an intelligent and courageous woman, who also happens to be an actress from Babylon 5 and a former Playboy model who was Dodi Al Fayed's love interest before Princess Diana was. I don't make this stuff up folks.

But as much as I respect Christian, I had to ask myself, what are the agendas at work here, when a lady I can watch on TV in an episode of Criminal Minds is also my primary source of information for medical treatment options for a significant medical illness? I imagine she probably wonders this herself.

I also came to the conclusion that the group that I had thought were the knights in white armor when it came to addiction—namely AA—has sadly been part of the problem—a big part.

Instead of taking a page out of the playbooks of other not-for-profits like the Heart and Stroke Foundation or the Susan G Koman Breast Cancer Foundation, AA sticks to its own 1930s playbook—the 'Big Book'—and refuses to acknowledge any medical treatment that didn't exist in 1939.

And evil pharma? They aren't evil in this story—they've mostly stayed away from the wholly unprofitable mess, waiting for AA-thinking to loosen its hold and doctors to decide to start treating alcoholism like any other illness.

So now you know a little about what's new today, the state we are in, and some of the players that got us to where we are today.

Next, I'll back up some of my claims about the effectiveness of the medication and the research behind it.

04 | SIX SAD TRUTHS

"I'm not trying to predict the future. I'm trying to let us see the present."

–William Gibson

JUST THE FACTS

As I read research report after research report about medications that can treat alcoholism, these facts became apparent:

1. There is an abundance of high-quality research that shows the effectiveness of medications for alcoholism.

2. Many of the medications are safe and FDA-approved, and as effective in alcoholism as other widely prescribed drugs are for other illnesses.

3. Research backing some of the medications has been in existence, and growing, for over a decade–if not longer.

4. Despite the lack of other effective treatments, the vast majority of alcoholics are not told about or prescribed these medications, even when they seek help.

5. The failure of medical professionals to prescribe drugs to alcoholics who need them has caused negative repercussions for future treatment innovations.

6. These issues have slowed down medical development–something which will have repercussions well into the next decade.

The first three points are good news for alcoholics and their families–there is hope–there is something you may not have tried.

But that fourth fact–that so many people are suffering and dying, and not being told about these options–is simply unacceptable.

The fifth and sixth statements–about negative repercussions–are something I'll delve into near the end of this chapter. But in a nutshell: when pharmaceutical companies can't sell good medications to those who need them, they stop developing them.

I'd like to back up those statements with data now, so let's look at some of the medications that you'll find more information about later in this book. Let's look at these five:

1. Acamprosate

2. Baclofen

3. Naltrexone

4. Topiramate

5. Gabapentin

These are five of the medications that are grouped into the A-List (Most Important Medications for Today), later in the book, where extensive detail is provided on each one.

FDA-APPROVAL

To achieve FDA-approval, a medication has to go through extensive testing. Safety is one of the many things tested.

These five medications are all FDA-approved—which means they have been shown to be safe in humans, and they are currently prescribed by physicians (mostly for other purposes).

Some of them are FDA-approved for alcohol addictions, and some achieved FDA-approval for a different illness.

All five in my list above have been FDA-approved for over a decade.

Here are the years in which they were approved and made available to doctors and patients:

- Acamprosate—11+ years of FDA approval (since 2004)

- Baclofen—38+ years of FDA approval (since 1977)

- Naltrexone—21+ years of FDA approval (since 1994)

- Topiramate—21+ years of FDA approval (since 1994)

- Gabapentin—13+ years of FDA approval (since 2002)

Years of Research for Alcohol Treatment

Of course, research into medications takes years before drugs reach the point of gaining FDA-approval.

When a drug is very new, with few years of research behind it, it is possible that there may be surprises around some of a medication's effects that have yet to be seen. That's why newer drugs deserve more caution than older ones.

But all five of the drugs we are examining here have been researched for years, again—over a decade even for the newest.

Here are the years when research began for each ones' effectiveness in alcoholism:

- Acamprosate: 30+ years of research (since 1985)

- Baclofen: 39+ years of research (since 1976)

- Naltrexone: 23+ years of research (since 1992)

- Topiramate: 12+ years of research (since 2003)

- Gabapentin: 15+ years of research (since 2000)

Number Needed to Treat (NNT)

An important term to know when evaluating the effectiveness of a medication is the medication's NNT–the Number Needed to Treat.

The NNT is the number of people that need to receive the medication before one individual is helped. So, for example, if a medication has an NNT of 10, it means that one in ten people treated with the drug is helped; or that the medication is effective 10% of the time.

The lower the NNT, the more people the medication is effective for.

To give you an idea of the relative effectiveness of medications for alcoholism it may be helpful to understand the NNTs for other common drugs.

Many medications commonly prescribed for depression have an NNT of around 5-10[1].

This means they help one out of every 5-10 people who take them. (And these are for the most effective anti-depressants—less often prescribed ones can have much higher NNTs).

Here are the NNTs for other often-prescribed drugs:[33]

- Antibiotics for sinusitis—1 in 15 are helped (an NNT of 15)

- Nicotine replacement to quit smoking—1 in 15 quit smoking (an NNT of 15)

- Antiplatelet agents (blood thinners) for stroke—1 in 79 are helped (an NNT of 79)

- Blood pressure medications (anti-hypertensives) to prevent death, heart attacks, and stroke—1 in 125 prevented death; 1 in 67 prevented stroke; 1 in 100 prevented heart attack (an NNT from 67-125)

- Daily aspirin to prevent first heart attack or stroke—1 in 1667 are helped (an NNT of 1667)

In comparison, the NNT numbers for the medications we're examining here for alcoholism have been found in research to be significantly lower (which means better):

- Acamprosate NNT: 1 in 7-12 are helped to reduce drinking or maintain abstinence (an NNT of 7-12)[134]

- Baclofen NNT: 1 in 3 are helped to reduce drinking or maintain abstinence (an NNT of 3)[35]

- Topiramate NNT: Unknown NNT

- Naltrexone NNT: 1 in 7-10 are helped to reduce drinking or maintain abstinence (an NNT of 7-10)[36]

- Gabapentin NNT: 1 in 5-8 are helped to reduce drinking or maintain abstinence (an NNT of 5-8)[37]

These NNT numbers are excellent–and not just for one of these drugs–all four of the drugs with known NNT numbers are the same or better than those of commonly prescribed medications doled out in doctors' offices every day.

Who gives medications their NNT numbers?

Scientists learn these numbers through repetitive research.

If you look at the small endnote numbers I've added as references you can trace them back to the bibliography at the end of this document and see the names of researchers, their research, and where the research was published.

You can then go to a search engine such as Google Scholar (scholar.google.com), search for the name and read it yourself.

QUALITY AND QUANTITY OF THE

BODY OF RESEARCH

For research to be deemed credible, one research paper isn't enough.

There has to be a 'body of research' for a medication to be considered credible.

So in other words, many well-published researchers, in many well-run research studies need to be able to consistently duplicate positive results for research to be considered highly credible and a medication to be regarded as effective.

Some individual studies can be so extensive and well-run that they carry a lot of weight by themselves, but usually a single study with new findings is of little significance until it can be reproduced by others.

There are also studies called 'Research Reviews' and 'Meta-analysis' which are useful too because these are 'studies of studies' which look at numerous individual studies of a particular drug to determine whether the entire body of research is conclusive.

Reviews and Meta-analysis are the aggregators of information in the world of research, and should be important sources of information for medical practitioners.

Many of the medications have such a body of research.

Here are statements from just a few of the papers:

For Acamprosate:

- There are "more than 450 published original investigations and clinical trials and 1.5 million treated patients which together has resulted in a convincing body of knowledge around acamprosate as an effective treatment for alcohol dependence."[38]

- The effectiveness of acamprosate is "robustly documented in meta-analyses of available studies...the latter of these was a meta-analysis of 17 studies which included 4087 individuals."[1]

- Acamprosate was found to be superior to placebo in the maintenance of abstinence in a 2015 study in patients with alcohol dependence. The 2015 report cited that "these findings concur with 11 randomized, blinded, placebo-controlled clinical trials conducted in Europe."[39]

- A 2012 analysis included 1317 women and 4794 men from 22 studies within 18 countries and found that acamprosate had "significant beneficial effect across 4 efficacy endpoints— percentage of abstinent days, the percentage of no heavy drinking days, the rate of complete abstinence and rate of no heavy drinking. Acamprosate also had a high rate of treatment completion and medication compliance.[40]

- A meta-analysis of data from 11 European clinical trials that included over 3000 showed that "acamprosate nearly doubled the likelihood of preventing relapse to drinking and increased the probability that patients would remain in treatment by nearly one-third."[41]

- In addition, acamprosate is available in at least 30 countries, including the United States, most of Europe, China, Singapore, and Australia, as well as Central and South American countries. It has been prescribed to over "1.5 million persons with alcohol abuse or dependence in those countries with no apparent pattern of serious side effects. European data indicate that the drug has no potential for abuse or rebound effect after discontinuation. European data have also indicated that the drug effectively reduces craving for alcohol and can help maintain abstinence in dependent patients."[42]

You don't have to be a rocket scientist to understand from those quotes that acamprosate should be on every doctor's radar.

Here are some research quotes for the others.

For baclofen:

- "The majority of clinical surveys conducted to date–including case reports, retrospective chart reviews, and randomized placebo-controlled studies–suggest the ability of baclofen to suppress alcohol consumption, craving for alcohol, and alcohol withdrawal symptomatology in alcohol-dependent patients."[43]

- "The constancy of improvement over the 2-years was remarkable...ninety-two percentage of patients reported that they experienced the craving-suppressing effect of baclofen."[44]

For topiramate:

- "There is now solid clinical evidence to support the efficacy of topiramate for the treatment of alcohol dependence."[45]

For naltrexone:

- "Meta-analyses of available trials, even when the negative study is included in the analysis, unequivocally support NTX [Naltrexone] efficacy"[1].

- "There is abundant evidence supporting the use of naltrexone for the treatment of alcohol dependence (Level A)."[41]

- As early as 2002, one report showed that up to 2001 there had already been 14 trials assessing the effectiveness of naltrexone compared with placebo for treating alcoholism, enrolling 2127 subjects, in five countries. It stated, "there is strong evidence that naltrexone significantly reduces alcohol relapses to heavy drinking, the frequency and quantity of alcohol consumption in those who do drink, and alcohol craving."[46]

- "Naltrexone is one of the most evaluated medications in clinical research for reducing craving. It was superior to placebo in lessening craving, preventing relapse to heavy drinking, and in increasing the percentage of abstinent days."[47]

- "Oral and long-acting injectable naltrexone… are approved for treatment of alcohol dependence. Their availability and consideration of their use in treatment are now standards of high-quality care."[48]

And for gabapentin:

- In a review of six randomized controlled clinical trials lasting at least 4 weeks, the four largest trials showed "beneficial effects of gabapentin on at least one alcohol-related outcome measure."[49]

- A large, well-managed 6-year study found Gabapentin significantly improved rates of abstinence and no heavy drinking. Abstinence rate was 4.1% in the placebo group … and 17.0% in the 1800-mg group. The no heavy drinking rate was 22.5% in the placebo group … and 44.7% in the 1800-mg group.[37]

- "Gabapentin's effect on drinking outcomes is at least as large or greater than those of existing FDA approved treatments...plus it's the only medication shown to improve sleep and mood in people who are quitting or reducing their drinking, and it's already widely used in primary care."[50]

RESEARCHER CREDENTIALS

On the internet, anyone can come across a lot of questionable 'research', written by a lot of questionable 'researchers.' Snake-oil salespeople are in abundance online, unfortunately.

But the researchers who wrote the above statements, and who found and stand behind the NTT numbers are some of the most educated, most published, most respected scientists in the field of addiction research in the world at this time.

They work at the most respected institutions in the world and those statements have been published in the top scientific addiction and medicine journals. And less than 20 researchers were quoted. There are hundreds more, highly credible scientists who are on the research teams for these studies, as well as contributing to other research cited in this book.

A few of the individuals (whose names are also in the endnotes at the back of the book), and who led the research just cited include:

- Dr. Rainer Spanagel, Director of the Central Institute of Psychopharmacology at the University of Heidelberg

- Dr. Markus Heilig, M.D., Ph.D., Head of Neuroscientific Research, Linkoping University (former Chief of the Laboratory of Clinical Studies, and Clinical Director of the United States National Institute of Alcohol Abuse (NIAAA) Division of Intramural Clinical and Biological Research)

- Dr. Mark Egli, Program Officer, Division of Neuroscience and Behavior, National Institute on Alcohol Abuse and Alcoholism

- Dr. Susumu Higuchi, MD, Ph.D., Director, National Hospital Organization, Kurihama Medical and Addiction Center, Japan

- Dr. Barbara Mason, Director, Laboratory of Clinical Psychopharmacology and Pearson Center for Alcoholism and Addiction Research

- Dr. Phillippe Lehert, Senior Consulting Statistician at United Nations, University of Melbourne

- Dr. M. Soyka, Head of the Department of Forensic Psychiatry of the Psychiatric Hospital of the LMU Munich

- Dr. Roberta Agabio, Head of the Centre for the Study of Adolescent Alcohol Dependence, Italy

- Dr. Renaud de Beaurepaire, Psychiatrist and neurobiologist, head of Psychiatry at the Paul Guiraud Hospital

- Dr. Bankole Johnson, Chair of the Department of Psychiatry, University of Maryland School of Medicine

- Dr. Nassima Ait Daoud Tiouririne, MD, Associate Professor in the Department of Psychiatry and Neurobehavioral Science and director of the Center for Addictions Research and Education, UVA

- Dr. Stewart Leavitt, MA, Ph.D., Addiction Treatment Forum Researcher/Editor

- Dr. Carolina L Haass-Koffler, Postdoctoral Fellow, Center for Alcohol and Addiction Studies, Brown University

- Dr. Adron Harris, Director of the University of Texas Waggoner Center for Alcohol and Addiction Research

- Dr. Morgan D. Greutman (Pharm D.) Southwestern Oklahoma State University

- Dr. Lorenzo Leggio, M.D., Ph.D., M.Sc., Chief of Clinical Psychoneuroendocrinology and Neuropsychopharmacology, NIAAA/NIDA

- Dr. George A. Kenna, assistant professor, Psychiatry, Center for Alcohol and Addiction Studies, Brown University, and a senior scientific advisor, Tufts Health Care Institute Program on Opioid Risk Management

If my life was at stake, that is a list of people that I would trust. And I'd want my doctor to trust them too.

How about you?

PUBLICATION QUALITY

Lending even more credibility to the researcher findings are the peer–reviewed journals where their work is published.

The statements and NNTs quoted above were published in highly respected, peer-reviewed journals, including these ones: Neuropsychopharmacology, Pharmacology and Therapeutics, American Psychiatric Association Journal, The Journal of Clinical Psychiatry, Alcoholism: Clinical and Experimental Research, World Federation of Societies of Biological Psychiatry, Frontiers in Neuroscience, Frontiers in Psychiatry, Current Pharmaceutical Design, CNS Drugs, Alcoholism: Clinical and Experimental Research, Journal of Pharmacy Technology, and JAMA (Journal of the American Medical Association).

I hope that briefly these sections have helped to illustrate my points about the quality of the body of research that has developed supporting the use of these medications for alcohol addiction treatment.

And that's just a small sampling–a *minute* sampling–of the much larger body of research that exists.

LACK OF OTHER EFFECTIVE TREATMENT

There are other kinds of (non-pharmaceutical) treatments available for alcoholics. The best known of these other approaches is Alcoholics Anonymous, which is discussed extensively later.

But this book is about 'evidence-based medicine'. Or, in other words, treatments that have a substantial body of research backing them.

Evidence-based medicine is the foundation of modern medicine and the only kind of medicine that should matter to licensed doctors who wish to avoid malpractice suits.

Some treatments certainly have an incredibly extensive body of *anecdotal* support (both for and against them), but judged in terms of raw, scientific data, other treatments have very little conclusive scientific support.

When we look at evidence-based medicine, there are no other treatments for alcoholism that have as strong a body of research backing them as do the medications I identified above.

Other treatments—which consist of either 12-step programs or behavioral therapy, have a 70-90% relapse rate.[51]

One of the most highly respected organizations in the world when it comes to meta-analysis' discussed earlier is an organization called Cochrane. Cochrane reviews are trusted worldwide for their credibility, impartiality, and extremely high quality.

There have been several reports and reviews published by Cochrane that support many of the medications discussed in the book. However, they also concluded in a 2006 review of studies going back to the 1960s that:

> *"No experimental studies unequivocally demonstrated the effectiveness of AA or [12-step] approaches for reducing alcohol dependence."[5]*

The report explicitly stated:

> *"People considering attending AA or TSF [Twelve Step] programmes should be made aware that there is a lack of experimental evidence on the effectiveness of such programmes."[5]*

The fact is, these treatments fail—for most people, most of the time.

Because of the lack of published data supporting other approaches, the US government has publicly backed Medication Assisted Treatment.

The US Government's Center for Substance Abuse Treatment, Substance Abuse and Mental Health Services Administration (SAMHSA) published a guide written for physicians and healthcare professionals in 2013, stating:

> *"Medication-assisted treatment has shown much promise in reducing alcohol use and promoting abstinence in patients diagnosed with alcohol use disorder.*
>
> *Considerable research evidence and consensus among experts support the use of pharmacologic treatments... A number of FDA-approved medications have been shown to be important elements of such treatment.*
>
> *"Although some patients do not benefit from medication-assisted treatment, most do.*
>
> *For each patient deemed an appropriate candidate for medication-assisted treatment, multiple pharmacologic agents offer a variety of options so that treatment can be tailored to each patient's needs and circumstances."[7]*

A Decade Ago, Alcoholics

Weren't Told

Earlier I discussed how many years the most important medications have been researched for, and how long they have been FDA-approved.

So it should be quite clear that none of the most important drugs I have identified in this chapter are new.

And while there is new research every day, which builds the case for their effectiveness, there was already abundant evidence of the efficacy of some of them many years ago.

Not only did evidence exist over a decade ago of their effectiveness, but it was also red-flagged by prominent researchers ten years ago that effective medications were not making it to the people who needed them most.

For example, nearly a decade ago, Mark Heilig and Markus Egli wrote a paper on behalf of the National Institute of Alcohol Abuse and Alcoholism (NIAAA) identifying the fact that even addiction medicine specialists were failing to prescribe drugs, such as naltrexone, that could help alcoholics.

It was clear that alcoholics just weren't receiving prescriptions for the life-saving medications they were researching.

For example, in 2007, in the United States, only about 720,000 prescriptions were written for alcohol treatment medications, representing approximately 78 million dollars in sales.

Compare that to the sales volume for the antidepressant Lexapro, generating 1.7 billion dollars in 2004, even though the number of US adults suffering from major depression is similar to those suffering from alcohol use disorder.[52]

Stepping beyond their usual clinical scientific demeanor, of naltrexone, the two highly respected scientists wrote:

> *"It is highly disturbing that this drug is not made available to the patients that need it."*[1]

They echoed the sentiments stated the year before, in 2005, when the American Council on Alcoholism pointed out:

> *"In other areas of medicine, it is highly probable that the development of such efficacious medication would prompt physicians to use it readily," but that in the area of addiction medicine, patients were not being treated with the efficacious medications that already existed.*[53]

TODAY, ALCOHOLICS STILL AREN'T TOLD ABOUT MEDICATIONS

Today, alcoholics *still* aren't being prescribed these safe, effective drugs that could save their lives.

We learned earlier that the NTT numbers for the most important medications today are similar to the NTT for most antidepressants.

The prevalence of depression and anxiety disorders is two or three times that of alcohol dependence. However, antidepressants are prescribed 100 to 200 times as often as medications for alcohol dependence.[54]

SAMHSA's guide, referred to above stated:

> *"Although many experts in addiction believe that patients with moderate or severe alcohol-related problems should be offered medication-assisted treatment (MAT) on a routine basis, considerable resistance to the use of MAT persists..."*[7]

The resistance of health-care professionals to prescribe them has resulted in dismal numbers: multiple sources support numbers ranging from only 3-11% of those who need it receiving any kind of treatment.

One important 2012 study found:

> "Analysis indicates that only one in 10 (10.9 percent, 2.5 million) of those in need of addiction treatment (excluding nicotine) receive it, leaving a treatment gap of 20.7 million individuals."[3]

And the same report attacked the medical system, saying,

> "There simply is no other disease where appropriate medical treatment is not provided by the health care system and where patients instead must turn to a broad range of practitioners largely exempt from medical standards."[3]

Addiction medicine is simply the ugly sister of the world of medicine.

Dr. Shelly Greenfield, Director at the Harvard Medical School, has singled out addiction medicine, stating:

> "There is no other comparable example in medicine where you have evidence-based treatments that are not available.[3]

A 2014 report published in the American Journal of Psychiatry confirmed the 2012 report's points, stating explicitly that "a recent study of Veterans Health Administration facilities showed that nationally, only 3% of Veterans Health Administration patients with alcohol use disorder received treatment medications."[2]

The authors echoed earlier sentiments once again, stating:

> "There is an enormous gap between the number of alcohol use disorder patients who would potentially benefit from medications and the number of patients who actually receive medications."[2]

Elsewhere in the world, treatment seeking alcoholics are little better off.

In the United Kingdom, the vast majority (80-95%) receive no treatment[55], and the few medications that are most often prescribed are limited to only three early medications—disulfiram, acamprosate, and naltrexone—instead of the wider options now shown to be effective.

In comparison with other kinds of mental illness, alcohol addiction has the broadest treatment gap of all mental disorders, since 82% of people with schizophrenia, 60% of people with bipolar disorder and 55% of people with major depression receive treatment versus the dismal 8% of people with alcohol dependence that need and receive treatment.[5556]

So clearly, my fourth point—that despite the lack of other effective treatments, the vast majority of alcoholics are not told about or prescribed these medications, even when they seek help—is clear.

And that sums up the situation we are in today: Alcoholism—the world's most deadly disease[8] can be treated with lots of life-saving, promising, safe, FDA-approved medications...but nobody is getting them.

A LOST DECADE FOR DRUG DEVELOPMENT

If that isn't bad enough, it gets worse.

When promising, well-supported medications are researched, known about for over a decade, and then *never* make it into the hands of the patients that need them, there are negative repercussions: research and development 'get stuck.'

In 2006, Heilig wrote a roadmap for the next generation of development for drugs to fight alcohol addiction.

In it, he identified three waves of pharmacological treatments.

The first wave–already heavily researched and FDA-approved by 2006–included disulfiram, naltrexone, and acamprosate.

He predicted a second wave of drugs that would improve efficacy and allow more tailored treatment, taking genetic makeup into account. The second wave would include drugs like ondansetron, baclofen, and topiramate.

The third wave would target systems in the brain already identified as holding much potential for treatment using new, yet-to-be-named medications.[1]

Heilig's three waves may have seemed overly optimistic–but they weren't. His roadmap merely represented the great promise that existed (and still exists) for the treatment of alcohol addiction.

Heilig was correct in his predictions about which drugs and targets would be important in the coming years.

But today, unfortunately, the government is still trying to get the medical community on board to prescribe even the very first wave of drugs.

And the appetite of pharmaceutical companies to shepherd the second and third waves through expensive clinical trials, is weak at best.

When pharmaceutical companies can't sell effective drugs they have spent millions of dollars developing–like naltrexone for example–they stop investing (or they fail to start in the first place). After all, why would a pharmaceutical company risk investment in new drugs, when the old, proven ones, sat on shelves?

So instead of the second and third wave of medications getting pushed through to the FDA-approval stage, only the first wave got over that hump.

The second wave is FDA-approved–but for other illnesses.

And the third wave is having difficulty getting out of the pre-clinical research stage.

It's been a lost decade in research and development for addictions.

DRUG PIPELINE IS DRY

We can see the impact of this lost decade in the drug pipeline, which is the name for the process that drugs follow to get from discovery to FDA-approval.

In the drug pipeline is the set of substances that pharmaceutical companies have in discovery or development at any given time.

On average, each year in the United States, 25 drugs finish their journey through the pipeline and are given FDA approval.

It can take 10-15 years and millions of dollars in investment for a drug to progress from the beginning through to the end of the drug pipeline.

The drug development cycle is so long that if there is a period of a decade when the drug pipeline slows down, that slowdown will negatively impact drug development well into the future.

Last year in the United States, a bumper crop of 41 new drugs made it through to attain approval.

Several (four) of these were for type 2 diabetes, four were antibiotics and five were for cancer treatment.

And over 40 percent—or 17 of the new drugs were for rare diseases—diseases that affect 200,000 or fewer Americans.[57]

If each of these rare diseases affected 200,000 Americans, it would mean that at most 3.4 million Americans could now be treated with these new drugs.

But at least five times the number of Americans (18 million)[14] suffer from alcohol dependence—and not a single drug was approved last year to treat these Americans.

Nor the year before, nor the year before.

Despite the great work researchers have done in understanding the illness, and the enormous need for medical treatment, not a single drug has been approved for the treatment of alcohol dependence in the United States for over 10 years.

Nor is it likely that this trend will change soon.

In April 2014, there were 113 substances registered in human clinical trials for the treatment of any type of mental illness.

Of these 113, only four were in human trials specifically for the treatment of alcohol dependence.

Only 20% of drugs going through clinical trials ever progress to FDA Approval, so for the odds to work in their favor, at least 23 of the drugs in clinical trials right now would have to be targeted to alcohol dependence for one of them to achieve FDA approval.

With only four at that level right now, the chances are small that we will see a new drug for alcohol dependence in the next five years.

And those, my friend, are the sad truths about medications for the treatment of alcoholism.

05 | THE PLAYERS

"If you have hypertension and it flares up, you go to a specialist. The specialist doesn't discharge you to a church basement.

If he did, we would call it malpractice."[58]

—Psychologist Thomas McLellan, University of Pennsylvania

ALCOHOLISM CULTURE

If you are reading this book, the chances are that you, like me, live in a first world country.

I used to naively presume that one of the benefits of such privilege was that drugs that work would automatically be channeled to the people that needed them. That isn't the case with alcoholism though.

To understand why, we need to look at a broad, amorphous collection of issues and groups which I lump into a category I call 'alcoholism culture'.

All major diseases have their own unique culture. Look at the Google image search results when you search for the name of a disease and you'll see a visual depiction of that culture.

For example, breast cancer culture is defined by the pink ribbon, and imagery of 'survival.' The face of breast cancer is predominantly female. Imagery and copy carries a tone of hope, conquer, walking for the cure! And power in numbers! (And excessive use of enthusiastic exclamation marks!)

In contrast, alcoholism culture appears in shadows and dark colors. It's more masculine. There are images of handcuffs and alcohol and people sitting in shadows and garbage. The tone is overwhelmingly that of desperation and a loss of dignity.

Every disease culture has its issues. Documentarian Ravida Din looked at breast cancer culture and made a movie about its dark side (Pink Ribbons Inc.).

Her work highlighted how some major corporations use the pink ribbon on products to increase sales while donating only a tiny fraction to the cause. The movie illustrated how women are encouraged to participate in cheerful pink pep rallies instead of tackling harder issues.

Din says, "the question I was intrigued by was, 'How did we get to this kind of breast cancer culture that privileges shopping [as a solution] as opposed to getting angry and asking for change?'"[59]

We might take a page out of Din's book and ask, "How did we get to this kind of alcoholism culture where doctors send patients to a religion-based program that fails 90% of the time, as opposed to getting angry and asking for change?"

Din says, "I want people to learn to ask questions…I want to change the discourse which has been the same for decades, and to see what we can do to be more efficient to counter this terrible disease."[59]

We have to ask the same questions about alcoholism.

Because if how we are tackling breast cancer is *'inefficient'*, how we tackle alcoholism is downright backwater inept.

And we can't improve on the system we have unless we find its weaknesses.

Din looked at the key groups involved to find their inefficiencies. And that's where we need to look too.

This chapter looks at alcoholism culture's stakeholders and the roles they play.

If, as Din says, 'we need to learn to ask questions', then it's these groups those questions need to be directed to.

ALCOHOLICS ANONYMOUS

AA is a community of individuals who are struggling with a devastating, lonely, isolating disease. To its members, AA offers companionship, support, love, the opportunity to grow through helping others, and a system for living a moral, positive lifestyle.

The support provided to alcoholics by fellow AA members can be overwhelmingly positive, and for those individuals who are assisted in overcoming addiction by relying on that support and the AA system, AA can be nothing short of miraculous and life altering.

But as great as AA is in many ways, it is also a problem.

In fact, it's the biggest problem.

It's this single stakeholder that has been the most influential and detrimental to the advancement of medical treatment for alcoholism.

It spreads mistruths and myths that block our understanding of what science now holds to be true.

Its influence is behemoth.

Its viewpoints form the cultural backbone of alcohol addiction treatment throughout the world.

Without donating a dime to research, it has profoundly influenced the medical profession and become the basis of expensive treatments at a plethora of treatment centers and rehab programs.

And it doesn't even work.

Its turnover rate is massive, and its failure rate is estimated around 90%.

•••

AA's originator—Bill Wilson—died over 40 years ago in 1971. His death occurred more than a decade *before* the first medications for the treatment of alcoholism were first discovered and more than twenty years before ideas about evidence-based medical treatment began to appear.

To say AA is a unique organization is an understatement. It has a culture unto itself and it has been pointed out by many critics that it shares characteristics similar to cults.

But that doesn't really matter, because that's not the issue.

If it were a cult that actually was a statistically proven, effective treatment for addiction and encouraged the advancement of effective medical treatment, then I'd probably applaud it.

EVIDENCE-BASED MEDICINE

"The wisdom to know the difference."

—*Last line of the Serenity Prayer*

In the fall of 1974, a doctor named Dr. David M. Eddy was asked to give a talk about how physicians make decisions.

Eddy decided to write about diagnostic mammography. He thought he would find "strong evidence, good numbers, and sound reasoning."

But to his amazement he found "very few numbers, no formal rationale, and blatant errors in reasoning."[60]

So he decided to look at another treatment, one that had been used for more than 75 years for ocular hypertension.

"Tens of millions of people were receiving it; surely there would be solid trials to support those decisions."

But to Eddy's dismay, he found just the opposite–only eight controlled trials had been conducted–all small and poorly designed.

"But perhaps the most startling, six of the eight trials showed that patients got worse with treatment, not better."[60]

Eddy tried to look at yet a third medical treatment but experts he consulted told him there wasn't enough evidence or data to do an analysis.

Wrote Eddy, "that clinched it. If there wasn't sufficient information to develop a decision tree, what in the world were physicians basing their decisions on? I then realized that medical decision making was not built on a bedrock of evidence or formal analysis, but was standing on Jell-O.[60]

Eddy spent much of the rest of his career contributing to an area now called 'Evidence-Based Medicine.'

Evidence-Based Medicine is the philosophy that says that doctor's treatment choices need to be based on solid proven data about the potential outcomes of those choices.

It is now widely recognized by medical associations, educators, physicians and insurance companies as the gold standard for determining what is and is not solid, defendable medical care.

In just 40 years, this approach has changed the way decisions are made about treatment in every single field of medicine.

Every single field of medicine that is, except the treatment of alcoholism.

•••

When it comes to addiction medicine, the majority of physicians, hospitals, treatments centers and other caregivers advise patients to pursue an 80-year old treatment which has never had any quantitative research evidence to support it.

And even worse, instead of helping alcoholics get proper medical care, Alcoholics Anonymous participants dissuade fellow members from taking medications that can help them treat their alcoholism.

In his recent book, *The Sober Truth: Debunking the Bad Science Behind 12-Step Programs and the Rehab Industry*, Dr. Lance Dodes, a retired psychiatry professor from Harvard Medical School, used data from more than 50 studies[6] to show AA's success rate is probably somewhere between 5 and 8 percent.[61]

In 2006, the Cochrane Collaboration, a health-care research group that produces some of the most respected meta-studies in medicine today, reviewed studies going back to the 1960s. They found that "no experimental studies unequivocally demonstrated the effectiveness of AA or [12-step] approaches for reducing alcohol dependence or problems."[5]

But a decade later, doctors are still sending patients there. And that's dangerous.

No Data

"With no other affliction, and with no other disadvantaged group, would such a pathetic outcome be deemed a success."[11]

—Dr. Peter Ferentzy, Addiction Scientist

Despite the lack of evidence for AA, members continue to support it.

They do so vigorously, emphatically, passionately, with great loyalty, sometimes angrily, but with no supporting empirical data whatsoever.

AA does not track the success of its members.

AA could take some of their book royalties and fund a major, international, scientific research study, run by respected third party scientists, from respected institutions, that unequivocally shows that it is helping people.

By helping its supporters with credible data, AA could help more alcoholics.

But AA has not done this and has shown no interest in doing so.

To justify why no transparent, credible data is produced for outside critics, its members hide behind the tenth tradition that instructs, AA "has no opinion on outside issues; hence the A.A. name ought never be drawn into public controversy."

But lack of credible data achieves just the opposite–AA supporters passionately and publicly advocate for the program while falling back on research shown to be flawed and biased.

It creates a heated and meaningless dialogue and pulls the AA name into controversy, whether they like it or not.

For example, take a 2013 Huffington Post article written by author and AA advocate Anna D.

She stated, "words like 'evidence-based' treatment are thrown around, and that certainly sounds like something wise and logical, especially when measured against an anonymous organization that has never and does not plan to track its membership numbers or the success of those members."

But then, despite her criticism of the idea of evidence-based treatment, Anna D. goes on to reference a 2005 study that was according to her "the largest study ever done on the topic, out of Stanford..." The study "reported that there were 33 percent higher success rates for AA participants than non-AA participants at the 16-year follow-up mark."

Unfortunately, the "largest study ever" cited by Anna D. was conducted by a researcher that critics have called a 'professional propagandist for the 12-Step treatment industry.'

Five years before Anna D.'s 2013 article, a report was published in the *International Journal of Mental Health and Addiction* which reviewed other pro-AA 'studies' including five studies by the author of the study that Anna D. cited.

It thoroughly discredited the research, stating that it was "based on studies lacking a no-treatment control ... infused with extraneous and discordant conceptual elements."

It said, "this design could not constitute a legitimate evaluation of the effectiveness...clearly there was no scientifically valid evaluation."[62]

In less scientific terms, according to one critic, the research was "invalid, erroneous, badly done, and downright deceptive and faked."[63]

Even if the study Anna D. cited had been meticulously run, the author's credibility had already been destroyed. So why even quote him?

Because even a Huffington Post writer couldn't find anything better.

The example of Anna D. and the flawed study is not a unique one. It is illustrative of the quality of the emotion-laden debate that rages on between AAs' loyal supporters and those who are less supportive.

So instead of focusing on solutions, while people die, mudslinging triumphs.

All evidence is purely subjective and unqualified.

Did it work for Anna D? Do you think AA works? Do I think it works? Do we know people it worked for? Does my doctor like it? Has he been recommending it for years? Does it make you feel good? Did it help your mom? Do I like it? Do you like it?

If there's no quantitative research supporting it, then it doesn't matter what you or I think, because the practice of medicine is no longer based on subjective opinion in this century.

No data, no can do.

The bottom line is that if one of the world's most highly respected research review organizations, the Cochrane Collaboration, can't find evidence to support its efficacy, then any doctor claiming to practice good medicine should not be recommending it.

End of discussion.

IS AA DANGEROUS?

How is AA dangerous?

Dodes put it so succinctly:

> *"I'm not trying to eliminate AA...I'm just saying it should be prescribed to that tiny group who can make use of it.*
>
> *It's terribly harmful when you send 90 percent of the people for the wrong treatment advice."*[6]

So perhaps there is no research data proving AA is helpful. But can it really be dangerous?

Yes—it really is 'terribly harmful'.

One reason it is harmful is because it actively deters, even shames members who wish to take medication to treat their addiction. And that's deadly.

To underline this point, let's go back to Anna D.'s article again.

IT'S HARMFUL

The topic of Anna D.'s original article was her outrage over the partnering of Hazelden (a treatment organization rooted in 12-steps that recently adopted medication assisted treatment), and the

Betty Ford clinic (a treatment organization that had not adopted medication as part of treatment).

These two organizations were the two most respected, best-known names in the private recovery-business before they merged.

She wrote, "if the recent news results in a conglomerate that owns both Betty Ford and Hazelden and supports medication-assisted treatment, that would be a *tragedy of unspeakable proportions.*"

Or in other words, she was expressing her view that treatment for addicts that includes medication is a tragedy worth getting really angry about. Her view underlines the view of many AA members and supporters.

Two years later, in January 2015, another article was published in the Huffington Post–an article by Jason Cherkis called, 'Dying to be Free.'[64]

This time, HuffPost carefully examined the treatment histories of 93 people who died of drug overdoses after treatment.

They found that the majority of the dead had participated in 12-step programs that dissuaded them from taking FDA-approved medications that would help them manage cravings for drugs.

The newly clean addicts graduated from treatment, committed to drug and medication-free abstinence.

But soon their addictions caught up with them, and with nothing to fall back on to help them control the cravings that are symptomatic of addiction, they overdosed, and died.

Cherkis concluded that the philosophy of the 12-step abstinence approach directly contributed to the deaths of the 93 addicts.[28]

Had they been taking medication, many of the deaths may not have occurred.

Instead of arguing (as had Anna D.) that treatment with medication was an 'unspeakable tragedy,' Cherkis argued that *12-step treatment, without medication,* had *caused* an unspeakable tragedy.

•••

AA was once a convenient, even romantic (and highly romanticized) idea.

We've been seeing this romanticized, clichéd view of AA for years in movies and on TV. I can't watch a crime drama without seeing the scene where the cop with the secret addiction attends the program after a stressful day on the job.

And in one of those paradoxical moments that occur in life from time to time, even actress and the naltrexone advocate mentioned earlier (Claudia Christian) once starred in a movie featuring AA.

She played a young addict in the major Hollywood blockbuster 'Clean and Sober' alongside Michael Keaton and Morgan Freeman.

According to the description of the movie (I suggest you say this out loud in that deep announcer voice for full effect), "a hustling drug addict checks himself into rehab to escape trouble with the law, and realizes that it's *exactly what he needs.*"

We love the idea of AA and have long been happy to send alcoholics there without question. It's *exactly what they need*, isn't it?

But now, as we saw with the deaths of the 93 freshly sober addicts, AA's philosophies are clearly *interfering* with—not operating in tandem with—medical treatment.

OPIATES AND ALCOHOLISM: A CLARIFICATION

Yes, it is true that the Cherkis story was about deaths from drug overdose; and yes, this is not the same as alcohol abuse.

And much of the brand new approach we are now seeing around addiction treatment led by the Obama administration is being driven not by the epidemic of alcoholism, but by rising numbers of deaths of drug addicts (which evidence shows are helped more effectively by medication than by 12-step programs.)

Couldn't it be argued that drug addiction and alcohol addiction are two completely different things?

There isn't as much of a distinction here as you might think.

All chemical addictions–whether from a pill, an injection, or a bottle–are fundamentally the same–they create a chemically-triggered series of adaptations in the brain that erode critical circuits.

And 12-step programs–whether for drug or alcohol addiction–are also fundamentally the same: they are religion-based programs that encourage an abstinence philosophy that dissuades participants from using medication to assist them in sobriety.

The only difference is that when 12-step programs don't work for drug addicts, the outcome is faster and more jarring than the outcome for alcoholics.

Drug addicts can seem healthy, hopeful and promising one day as they walk out of 12-step programs clutching their 12-step literature.

And then they die abruptly with a needle in their arms the next.

The tragic demise of young drug addicts (like TV's Glee star Cory Monteith, dead a few months after leaving rehab in 2013) is devastating and dramatic, and when it happens in great enough numbers (as it is now in the United States), it begs attention and investigation.

But when alcoholics die (after 12-step programs fail them too, sometimes over and over again), there is rarely a swift death (except suicide, which carries its own secretive stigma).

Alcoholics die slowly, agonizingly, quietly.

By the time they die, they no longer hold the promising, hopeful glow that clean young drug addicts carry. Like scrubbed birds, they lick their wounds and die quietly, alone.

The connection between the failure of the AA program they attended, and their eventual deaths is blurred by time and age.

THE SHIFT

The headlines I wrote about near the beginning of this book illustrate society's evolution toward medically assisted treatment, and away from our love affair with 12-step programs.

And in two short years, these Huffington Post articles–and their strongly diverging viewpoints from the same publication–show the same shift.

A third article–an October 2015 piece in Huffington Post–further crystallizes this change.

It reported:

> *"The treatment industry overwhelmingly resists a medication-assisted model based on decades-old beliefs about sobriety that have been passed down by those in recovery, but have never been rigorously tested.*[28]

It stated that for decades treatment had "ignored the scientific consensus that the best approach involved medications approved by the Food and Drug Administration, coupled with counseling."

It reported that "instead, the treatment industry insisted on a model known as 'abstinence,' in which any prescription medication aimed at addressing a patient's opioid use disorder was forbidden."[28]

That article shows a change of direction, but one of the most telling phrases–the one that jumps out at me–is this: "a model known as 'abstinence'."

There is something about this new phrase that sticks out like a sore thumb in the subtle way it creates distance and doubt between proper medical treatment and the 12-step approach.

Instead of Anna D.'s loving reference to AA programs as the 'gold standard of care'… for the first time, abstinence isn't the only way–it's simply 'a model'.

And not only that–but it's one that 'ignores scientific consensus' too.

ROOTS OF AA

BACK TO THE BEGINNING

Today, AA is large and powerful. The organization estimated in January 2012 that there were nearly 64,000 groups with 1.4 million members in the United States and Canada.

Worldwide, it's estimated there are more than 114,000 groups and 2.1 million members.[65] And AA's extremely high attrition rate means millions more have cycled through the doors of AA.

But that's just the tip of the iceberg for the number of people who have experienced AA's model, since AA's numbers don't include other 12-step based programs (which are essentially AA programs, without the AA name).

Twelve step programs, modelled on AA are the programs most recommended by doctors to patients with addiction. Even physicians with addiction receive 12-step based treatment for addiction 95% of the time.[66]

AA's influence is monolithic.

To understand how it got that way, we have to go back to the beginning.

•••

Bill Wilson was the genius behind AA. He systematized the recovery method that worked for him in 1935, and by doing so AA (and all other 12-step programs, including AA's family programs Alanon and Alateen) were born.

He and his cronies developed the 12 Steps, 12 Traditions and many more fundamental elements of the program and its unique, networked, ground-up organizational structure. It is a testament to his genius that it is still a thriving organization 44+ years after his death in 1971.

Yet while this iron infrastructure he built for the organization kept it strong for decades, it also encapsulated a fatal flaw: its complete inability to change and evolve.

There are very few things that are the same today, as they were in 1935. But one of the things that is very much the same is AA, and many AA members like it that way.

There is not only comfort in consistency and repetition, but the thinking is that since we don't really know what the 'magic sauce' is that supposedly helps so many people, changing any aspect might just change the program's potential for success—and nobody in AA wants that to happen.

Unfortunately, unknown to many AA members, Wilson did not want the organization to stop evolving.

The one element that even the visionary Wilson was unable to impart into AA's DNA was the ability for the organization to evolve and progress. And by the time he realized this, he had already lost control of the organization to its own strangely-networked structure.

AA COMMANDEERS THE MEDICAL COMMUNITY

One of the ways that Wilson shared the idea of AA with other alcoholics was through the medical community.

He and his fellow AA-members realized that if they reached just one doctor, that doctor would be able to contribute credibility as well as reaching many more alcoholics. Endorsement of AA by the medical community was crucial to its growth (as crucial back then as it is today).

Wilson (a brilliant salesman–but not a doctor) sold doctors on AA so well that if he were still alive today, he could teach classes to New York PR agencies.

He coddled them, he stroked their egos, he bowed down to them all, humbling himself, while selling them on AA.

He sold physicians of the day so hard that he practically made them believe the whole thing was their own great idea.

He called himself a 'drunk' and worshiped at their feet.

It was great salesmanship–not data–that sold the medical community on Alcoholics Anonymous.

He spoke around the world to doctors, and transcripts of those speeches still exist.

In one, he said:

> *"Now we come to the specialist, usually the psychiatrist. I'm glad to say that psychiatrists in great numbers are referring alcoholics to A.A. — even psychiatrists who more or less specialize on alcoholics. Their understanding of alcoholics is now great. Their patience and their tolerance of us, and of A.A., have been monumental.*
>
> *In 1949, for example, the American Psychiatric Association allowed me to read a paper on A.A. before a section of its Annual Meeting. As these doctors specialize in emotional disorders — and alcoholism is certainly one of them — this act of theirs has always seemed to me a wonderful example of fine humility and generosity. The reprints of even that one paper have had a vast effect, worldwide. I'm sure that we A.A.'s have never been sufficiently appreciative of all of this."*

And he said,

"It is very gratifying to know that today the subject of alcoholism is being taught in many of our medical schools. In any case, the facts about alcoholism are easy to obtain. Organizations like the National Council on Alcoholism, the Yale School of Alcoholic Studies, plus innumerable state rehabilitation and clinical efforts, are ready sources of helpful knowledge. So armed, the family physician can — as we say in A.A. — "soften up" the drunk so that he will be willing to take a look at our Fellowship. Or, if he balks at A.A., he may be directed to a clinic, a psychiatrist, or an understanding pastor. At this stage, the main thing is that he recognize his illness and that he start to do something about it."

"If the family physician's job is carefully done, the results are often immediate. If the first attempt doesn't work, the chances are better than even that persistent and successive approaches will bring results. These simple procedures do not rob the family physician of much time, nor will they be necessarily hard on the patient's pocketbook. A concerted effort of this sort by family physicians everywhere could not fail to achieve immense results. In fact, the effect of the family physician's work of this sort has already been great. And for this, I would like to set on our record the very special thanks of A.A. to them."[67]

Wilson's selling job came from the heart. He, like many people in the area of addictions who see people suffer from the disease, was compassionate and simply trying to help others in the best way he knew how.

The results of Wilson's selling job? His incredible influence on the medical community is still seen today.

It is estimated that 40% of members are referred by a doctor or other health care professional.[65]

And the medical community has invested itself in AA's 12-step approach so much, in fact, that it is the gold standard of care when it comes to treating their own.

Most Physician Health Programs (PHPs), which are attended by doctors with addiction problems, operate under the principles espoused by AA. Virtually all physicians are expected to attend AA or other 12-step meetings.[66]

One study looked at nearly 1000 physicians in PHP programs in the United States. It found that "regardless of setting or duration, essentially all treatment provided to these physicians (95%) was 12-step oriented, with a goal of total abstinence from any use of alcohol and other drugs of abuse and included the expectation of continued participation in AA or other 12-step oriented post-treatment support."[66]

In contrast, the study found that medication for the treatment of alcoholism was prescribed for only 5% of physicians.[66]

WILSON WANTED MEDICAL ADVANCEMENT

Wilson didn't want AA to become 'anti-medication'. But something happened over time.

Wilson knew AA was not the final solution for many alcoholics.

He wanted the medical community to buy into AA, but he also wanted the medical and research community to continue to look for treatments for alcoholics, and he wanted AA to support these efforts. This is something AA has conveniently forgotten.

He said in one speech:

> *"I would like to make a pledge to the whole medical fraternity that A.A. will always stand ready to cooperate, that A.A. will never trespass upon medicine, that our members who feel the call will increasingly help in those great enterprises of education, rehabilitation, and research which are now going forward with such promise."*[67]

He was well aware that AA wasn't a solution for everyone.

In 1961, he wrote, "It would be a product of false pride to claim that AA is a cure-all, even for alcoholism."[68]

In 1965, he even wrote a letter encouraging the "Dear Physicians of AA," to consider investigating niacinamide as a treatment for alcoholics.[69]

But the horse had already left the barn.

It's hard to sell the idea that AA is 'the solution' on one hand while encouraging science to seek better solutions on the other.

The founder of AA himself couldn't get anyone to listen. Wilson was as successful in his ability to influence the medical community as he was unsuccessful in influencing those in AA to support the medical and scientific advancement of addiction treatment.

Despite his pledge that AA would "stand ready to cooperate" in "those great enterprises of education, rehabilitation and research," the program was set in stone, and would continue to be for another eight decades.

And in practice, then, and today, other than integrating 12-step methodology firmly into most rehabilitation and treatment centers, there was no cooperation in the enterprises of education, rehabilitation and research.

DON'T MENTION MEDICINE

Despite Wilson's own wishes, today in the AA fellowship nobody talks about the implications of biochemistry on treatment. And nobody applauds the success of any other method than AA.

See for yourself: stand up in an AA meeting one day and talk about all of the advances in medical science when it comes to the treatment of alcoholism and see the response you receive.

Wilson might actually have applauded this, but most AA members don't know this, and certainly won't applaud you. You'll be rewarded with nasty looks, and pulled aside for 'a talking to' by old timers after the show.

Within AA, discussion of medical advances in the treatment of alcoholism is not allowed.

Now, those in AA will bristle at the use of the term 'not allowed'– you can talk about anything at AA–there are no written rules.

But the unwritten ones are numerous and conformity to them is heavily protected by a currency that is like lifeblood to isolated alcoholics–social inclusion.

Conformity means inclusion and non-conformity carries with it the risk of social rejection.

And it's well implanted in the heads of AA members that rejection from the group carries with it the risk of death.

I'm not over-exaggerating or making that up.

Death appears over and over again in AA's core tome (the Alcoholics Anonymous Big Book), and in another favorite book, 'Twelve Steps and Twelve Traditions (12 & 12)'.

It appears in phrases like: "unless each AA member follows to the best of his ability our suggested Twelve Steps of recovery, he almost certainly signs his own death warrant."

So any AA member talking about or recommending a pharmacological alternative to another alcoholic is quickly shunned and even excluded from the community—at great cost to the alcoholic, since AA may sometimes contain the only friends an alcoholic may have in the world.

STEP ONE IS NARCISSISM?

AA's complete lack of support of any kind of medical or research advancement is also very clearly seen in what it does not do: AA—the most powerful alcohol-treatment community in the world—has donated not one penny to medical research for the advancement of treatments for alcoholism.

It says so in the traditions: "An A.A. group ought never endorse, finance, or lend the A.A. name to any related outside facility or outside enterprise."

AA doesn't put money into prevention; it doesn't put money into medical research; it doesn't put money into the search for a cure or better treatment options. There's no pink ribbon for AA.

This is worth repeating again because it is a shameful truth of AA.

In 80+ years, AA has neither contributed nor endorsed the contribution of a single dollar to medical research. Not a dime. I hope someone will prove me wrong on this fact, because if you can, then that would be a wonderful precedent for AA to begin to do more.

In comparison, imagine if a group of cancer survivors refused to donate to cancer research, or the families of ALS sufferers declined to fundraise for ALS research.

In avoiding financial contribution, the message from AA is: the treatment we have is perfect; neither our fellow sufferers nor we need anything else.

That's unacceptable.

I have attended many AA meetings where at some point near the beginning, a somber announcement was made that an alcoholic–usually a young man–had died of alcoholism.

In any other community–people would ask, 'What can we do to help? How can we stop this from happening again and again? If so many people are dying, is what we have now really enough?!'

But at the end of the AA meeting, the chairs will be folded, the coffee pot washed, the ashtrays emptied, and everyone will go home.

AA collects money from its own members to keep the meetings going, and funds are generated through book sales, but no money is ever donated to the cause.

It begs the question: when an organization becomes as powerful as AA has become, is there not a *fundamental moral responsibility* to look at the role it plays in a wider community?

AA is a big black hole of alcoholics that do not contribute to finding medical solutions to their own disease.

How sad, how shameful, that such an influential organization has not used the strength of its membership to look for other ways to help its own.

If they had, perhaps this book would have been written 30 years ago and alcohol addiction would be something of the past.

THE AA EFFECT

Can a single non-medical organization like AA unintentionally change the way medical treatment for a disease has developed for decades?

Yes–for lack of a better term, I call it the AA Effect.

It works like this–

AA's influence extends outward to members, family, and friends. Eighty-year-old beliefs filtrate out to this wider circle. These beliefs define society's perspective of 'what is wrong with alcoholics' and how best to treat them.

The dominance of this influence on doctors, treatment programs, pharmaceutical companies and other key players in health care means other potential treatments and solutions aren't supported or funded.

The absence of endorsement is rejection; and so scientific and medical advancement starves, only inching along, instead of thriving.

And the direction of AA's influence is one-way only. There is no reverse osmosis. AA is impervious of and protected from influence from the opposite direction.

It achieves this insularity since anyone trying to change the group from within becomes a threat. Anyone who wants change is accused of wanting it because AA isn't working for them. But the message from the group is: 'If AA can't help you, there's no flaw in the system or change required. The flaw is in you and your weakness in following the program. Work harder.'

If an individual continues to push change, they are ostracized from the group. And because of this insularity and the non-emergence of any other viable alternative, the system remains strong and carries on.

Without knowing or intending to, AA has become a stifling force of nature deterring the kind of advancements in addiction medicine we've seen in the last 80 years in virtually every other area of medicine.

THE AA EFFECT AND MEDICATION

The full AA Effect can be seen playing out within the launch of one of the most important medications in this book—naltrexone.

Naltrexone is a medication that performed well in clinical trials, and then hit barrier upon barrier once released into the market.

It was originally synthesized in 1963 and patented in 1967 as 'Endo 1639A' by Endo Laboratories, a small pharmaceutical company in New York.

In 1969, DuPont purchased Endo Labs, and in 1972 the Special Action Office for Drug Abuse Prevention (SAODAP) was created by President Nixon. Director Jerome Taffe saw the development of naltrexone as one of his top priorities.

DuPont marketed the drug under the name 'ReVia'[70] after it obtained FDA approval in 1995 to market it for use in alcoholism.

The biggest barrier to marketing success is usually poor results in clinical trials. But in this case, clinical trials were successful. Data showed that the drug could work. (And in fact this is the very same drug that today—in a monthly-injection format—is finally getting market traction).

DuPont's problems began when they tried to market the medication to the medical and treatment community.

That's when they hit a wall.

Many doctors and alcohol addiction specialists were focused on AA as the only solution to alcoholism and wouldn't prescribe it.

DuPont faced an uphill battle just trying to convince providers that it was appropriate to treat addiction with a pharmacotherapy.[70]

DuPont failed.

Sales were dismal, and eventually The American Council on Alcoholism reportedly published the following scathingly worded statement on their website in 2005:

> *"Many physicians and non-physicians in treatment programs are unaware of the usefulness of naltrexone or how to use it.*
>
> *In other areas of medicine, it is highly probable that the development of such an efficacious medication would prompt physicians to use it readily.*

> *The biggest obstacle to using naltrexone for the treatment of alcoholism is the 'pharmacophobia' of many alcoholism-treatment professionals.*
>
> *This near-hysterical resistance to medication for treating alcoholism (or other substance-abuse disorders) has deep and tangled roots. Many recovering professionals learned in their recoveries that MDs and their prescription pads were evil purveyors of pharmacological lies and temptations.*
>
> *This attitude is often accompanied by a deeply rooted and strongly held belief that recovery has only one successful formula (usually the 12-step program) and that any modification to that approach is unethical.*
>
> *Scientific evidence is irrelevant to these individuals.*
>
> *They believe they have the 'truth' about recovery and don't want to be bothered with other points of view."*[70]

In 1997, ReVia's market exclusivity ended.

Other companies (Barr Laboratories and Bristol-Myers Squibb for example) began to sell generic naltrexone, but now, without the potential of high profitability, any pharmaceutical company producing it became very unlikely to market and promote it to a widespread audience.[53]

And today, not much has changed. Naltrexone (the pill form anyway) faces the same barriers.

Without profit potential, there is no naltrexone pill advertising campaign, no pharma sales reps talking to doctors about naltrexone; no free samples which doctors can stock and provide to patients; no information sessions or conferences about naltrexone for health care professionals.

It also means that in markets where drug companies choose to make it available, prices can be extremely high for those wishing to purchase it.

And this is why you will never see an ad for one of the most effective drugs to ever fight alcoholism in a TV commercial or on a poster in your doctor's office. This is why Claudia Christian is the person you are most likely to hear about naltrexone from.

Even worse, not only did AA-fueled medical resistance to evidence-based treatment of alcoholism cause naltrexone's launch to flop, but it cast a much wider shadow which would stunt research and development for decades.

Dupont's naltrexone flop taught pharmaceutical companies that doctors would not prescribe medication—even clinically-proven medication—as part of a treatment plan for alcoholics.

Pharmaceutical companies learned very well that the medical community, with its 'pharmacophobia' was sold on AA and only AA.

It is this lesson that has severely hampered pharmaceutical company investment in the business of alcohol addiction medicine ever since it was first learned.

Why would any pharmaceutical executive risk his or her career following in Dupont's footsteps to invest in or market any other alcohol addiction medication—even an incredibly effective one—when medical specialists and the sufferers of so many *other* diseases are crying out for new treatments?

That's why pharmaceutical company investment in the alcohol addiction pipeline has been nothing but a trickle for decades: And that's the AA Effect in action.

THE USUAL CLICHÉS AND STIGMA

FROM AA TO OUR LIVING ROOM

Peter Ferentzy is an outspoken research scientist at CAMH (the Canadian Association for Mental Health). He is also a historian of addiction, a recovering alcoholic and drug addict and the author of

'Dealing with Addiction–Why the 20th Century was Wrong'. His views are controversial, and right on the mark.

Ferentzy writes, "I'm sick of seeing people suffer needlessly and die needlessly. The assumptions upon which the North American approach to addiction is built... are mistaken, nasty, and stupid."[11]

A lot of these assumptions simply ooze right out of AA. It's like a wormhole from 1937 straight to our living rooms.

Without realizing it, they define our perspectives and our assumptions about what is wrong with alcoholics and how best to treat them.

Some of them pass through the rooms of AA into everyday language and become part of the zeitgeist-part of 'what we know' about alcoholics. Others are so questionable and strange that they haven't made it into society's vernacular.

•••

What we believe as a society is often held up to us in the mirror of pop culture, on TV shows and movies.

One of the reasons that the hit show *'Mad Men'* is so effective is because it reflects back to us beliefs held about men and women's roles in the 60s. The beliefs of the time jar so intriguingly with what we hold to be true today that it makes for a great backdrop to drama.

Society's beliefs around alcoholism and alcoholics, fed to us from AA, filter through via television and movies too.

Often we see the guy at the podium speaking humbly: "I needed an *attitude adjustment*. I finally *surrendered to my higher power* and *let go and let God*. I woke up at *rock bottom*, in a gutter and I decided to change."

These lines could slide easily into any TV drama. Yet they are incredibly damaging–and maybe in 20 years they will seem jarringly out of place too–as they should.

They are damaging because they imply that alcoholism is a moral failing and a shameful personality disorder, that requires severe punishment before it can be resolved.

Some of the clichés heard in AA rooms (what Ferentzy calls "powerful, culturally induced myths") include:

- "It's a spiritual malady."

- "Recovery from alcoholism requires a spiritual awakening from a higher power."

- "Rarely have we seen a person fail who has thoroughly followed our path."

- "The only solution to alcoholism is complete abstinence."

- "You've got to hit rock bottom."

Yet there is no medical or scientific data in existence that indicates that any of those myths are true.

Alcoholism is not caused by a bad attitude or planted in us by God. It is not the only illness in the world that is actually removable through a spiritual awakening. It is not something that requires the complete loss of dignity and surrender to recover from. It is not something that requires you to 'hit rock bottom' before you can recover.

Alcoholism is a mental illness. A brain disease. There are hundreds of scientific journal articles that back up this claim. If only someone would read them.

This section delves further into a few of these myths.

THE ALLERGY MYTH

One of the most ridiculous myths—well known and believed in AA, but not as often heard outside their doors—is the idea that alcoholism is an allergy.

Ask an AA alcoholic why they drink like they do and it's likely they will tell you they have an allergy to alcohol.

This big whopper is symbolic of all the other more subtle, more believable, equally outdated fallacies taught to alcoholics at AA.

In the 30s, when the big book was written, Bill Wilson's doctor, W.D Silkworth, explained to Wilson that alcoholism was an allergy.

He was not using the term as a metaphor. He was trying instead to use terminology to position alcoholism as an illness and explain its mechanism of action.

At the time, little more was known about allergies than was known about alcoholism. So the 'allergy explanation' was included in the AA Big Book and has remained there ever since–undisputed and uncorrected.[71]

Even the most recent 2001 edition supports the theory, stating: "As ex-problem drinkers, we can say that his explanation makes good sense."[72]

THE SPIRITUAL MALADY MYTH

AA members say their program is 'spiritual, not religious.'

Religious or not, whatever you want to label it, God is a significant part of the program, mentioned by name in four out of the 12 steps.

God in AA can be traced back at least to the early 1900s.

AA's early development was heavily influenced by an organization called The Oxford Group, which was an evangelical Christian movement that emerged in the 20s, growing up under the leadership of a Lutheran minister.

Bill Wilson always acknowledged that AA's spiritual and working principles came from this group.

The religious roots are reflected today in many elements of AA's approach. It appears not only in the phrase "spiritual malady," but also in the belief that a "spiritual awakening" must occur before abstinence is granted or made possible by one's "higher power."

AA describes alcoholism as a 'threefold disease' that combines the alcohol 'allergy', a "mental obsession", and a "spiritual malady."

AA teaches that when all three aspects are adequately addressed, addiction will 'lift'.

Alcoholics do have a mental obsession.

But they have a 'spiritual malady' that causes alcoholism, just about as much as they have an allergy.

CHARACTER DEFECTS & SHAME

The phrase 'spiritual malady' is often tied to another common AA concept and phrase—the idea that alcoholics are rife with 'character defects'.

AA teaches us: 'character defects' must be identified and remedied and where they have emerged at their worst, amends to others must be made.

Alcoholism is a medical illness. Yes, it has enormous repercussions to those with the disease—some of which emerge as what could be termed as character defects.

But character defects are by no means exclusive to alcoholics, nor do they cause alcoholism.

This misconception is damaging.

It leads to shame and stigma for the alcoholic and their family. It keeps our focus on alcoholics as the black sheep, instead of the ill family member.

As Markus Heilig wrote in a 2006 scientific journal:

"A medical approach to alcoholism treatment offers an established framework for developing and implementing evidence-based, rather than opinion-based treatment strategies.

An additional appeal of this approach is that it offers an alternative to moralizing and confrontational approaches, which are neither effective nor ethically attractive."[1]

ENABLING

AA and its sister organization for family and friends (Alanon) teach us that enabling is bad–that ALL negative consequences of drinking should be borne in full by the alcoholic.

In the 12-step world, any help you give to an addict that they wouldn't have needed if they didn't have an addiction in the first place is defined as enabling.

So, if an alcoholic needs ten dollars to buy another drink, and you give it to them, you are enabling.

If they need $50 to help cover their rent, and you give it to them, it is enabling.

If you give them a ride to detox, it is enabling. If they lost their license and need a ride to come join the family for Christmas dinner, giving them that ride is enabling.

We don't want to be enablers, so we don't give them the drink money, the rent money, the ride to detox or the ride to the family dinner.

And they go into withdrawal seizures, lose their apartment, hawk the watch that grandpa gave them to get a motel room for a night, and end up alone, sick, lonely, homeless and broken on Christmas day.

Merry Christmas.

The problem is that condemning all enabling behavior ignores the fact that people with addictions are human beings that are suffering and need connection, love and help, to get better.

It re-enforces the idea of rock bottom: that the more the person with an addiction is left to suffer and stew in their own mess, the more likely they will be to recover.

And this is not based on any kind of factual understanding of what might actually help someone begin to recover.

Sometimes, just the opposite is needed. In fact, when people recover, it is often a lot to do with the support they receive from family and friends.[11]

The three best predictors of success in recovery are[11]:

- Social support from family and friends

- Social standing–the things that give you esteem and dignity– like your job and your home

- Cognitive functioning–how well your brain continues to function

Notably, the first two elements–social support and social standing–are sometimes the two things that are taken away when we stop enabling.

And isn't it only a matter of time, for anyone, that when your social support and social standing are gone, your cognitive functioning starts to slip? Who can think rationally when they are lonely, cold, tired, degraded and sick?

Researchers say:

> *"Among alcoholics the recovery rates for one year are about 60 to 80% if you have both intact family and intact job. If you were missing one of those, it dropped in half to 30 to 40% after one year. If you were missing both, it drops in half again to 15 to 20%."*[73]

ROCK BOTTOM

The idea that an alcoholic must experience severe pain ('rock bottom') before they can recover is especially damaging.

Ferentzy writes of the ignorance of this perspective, saying:

> *"With no other medical condition—not even mental illness or neurosis—is the governing idea that the disease must be allowed to cause a great deal of damage in order to prepare someone for help"*[13]

He goes on to say:

> *"And this one stupid lie has—by means of treatment practice, social policy, societal attitudes, and even "wars" waged by politicians all over the world against drug users— killed millions and caused many more to suffer needlessly."*[13]

Friends of alcoholics are told not to create a crisis for the alcoholic—but not to avert one either. In other words, don't stand in the way of an alcoholic finally hitting rock bottom.

Well, many families wait and wait for that rock bottom to occur... and 3.3 million alcoholics every year finally hit rock bottom on the day they die from alcoholism.

For those that can't quit (that seem to bump along from rock to rock, unable to 'change'), many finally experience rock bottom at the end of a noose.

For very few, perhaps rock bottom does come with such massive pain that they are able to harness the last vestiges of control and mental focus they maintain.

But that massive pain can come in the form of killing someone while drunk driving, watching the faces of their children as child services take them away, spending Christmas alone with nobody and nothing… the lives that severe alcoholics live, while they wait for 'rock bottom' can be immensely painful.

Compassion For Addiction is an organization that was started by Vicky Dulai after her brother passed away.

She says, "Compassion and understanding when offering support must be constant. Addicts need not be punished, for they are already punishing themselves."

She also agrees that we must challenge the notion of 'rock bottom,' because "in my experience, rock bottom means death."[74]

Rock Bottom in the Medical System

Outside the family dynamic, we see 'rock bottom' formalized in the medical system.

Doctors, nurses, health care workers, the emergency room staff, detox center workers, police–the behaviors of many of the people that the alcoholic may need help from after relapse–are tainted with the notion that the alcoholic needs a measure of punishment upon discontinuation of drinking.

They may be doing their best; they may be caring, compassionate individuals; but sadly they are practicing an outdated, dangerous approach.

One place we see this is in detoxification facilities.

They are often unpleasant places where recovering alcoholics are treated more like naughty children or inmates than people with an illness.

Whereas other medical facilities help provide comfort to those in pain and discomfort, detox facilities are rarely equipped to provide, for example, medications which can lessen the intense physical discomfort felt by someone with an addiction. The more misery an alcoholic goes through when they detox, the better, it seems.

Medical care for people with alcoholism follows a different code. It's one that is silently, wordlessly justified by the myth of 'rock bottom.'

PURE ABSTINENCE

In a recent Newsweek article about medications for alcoholism, one longtime AA member was quoted as saying, "I'm not judging others, but for myself, using something like Vivitrol [naltrexone injection] or Campral [acamprosate] feels like a crutch ... It's not *true sobriety*."[58]

In alcoholism culture, you are either substance free, and counting your progress one day at a time, or you are failing.

And abstinence for AA–"true sobriety" does not include any of the medications in this book.

Oh, but remember: they aren't "judging others."

Abstinence or nothing is a very binary, black and white view of life. You are winning or you are failing–there's really no in-between.

But such black and white thinking is a set-up for failure. It doesn't work for most human beings.

One of the things 'all or nothing abstinence' leads to, is something called the 'Abstinence Violation Effect'–a dangerous phenomena.

The Abstinence Violation Effect was a term coined in 1980 by researchers Marlatt and Gordon. They noticed that a long-term relapse starts with just one drink.

That first drink (or small bout of drinking) was what they called a 'lapse.'

And they saw that whether the drinker continued from that first lapse to a full blown binge (a 'relapse') was highly dependent upon their emotional response to the initial lapse.[75]

Someone taught to believe that a lapse is a complete and utter personal failure, is likely to experience guilt and negative emotions that lead to increased drinking as a further attempt to avoid or escape their feelings and thoughts.

However, someone taught that a lapse is not a failure–just an opportunity to learn from one's mistakes–might not continue into full blown relapse.

It's the difference between blowing your diet for the next three weeks because you slipped up on one meal, or identifying that slip-up as a learning opportunity and applying the lesson to the next meal.

In contrast to other mental illness, one researcher says:

> *"We no longer blame people for sliding back into depressive states. We used to and were wrong to do so. Now, instead, we work within the depressive relapse to make it as painless as possible. That's the right approach. We must turn in that direction with addictions as well."*[11]

•••

Alcoholism culture is built around so many damaging notions: it's an allergy, you have a spiritual malady; you have a character flaw; relapse is failure; medication is weakness; punishment is helpful; if the program doesn't work for you, it's your fault; abstinence is the only way.

Perhaps many of these ideas were common outside AA in the thirties when the program first started. But as thinking around many other social issues changed with the times, these notions, incubated from change by AA, remained unquestioned.

And they continue to filter, year after year, into our zeitgeist.

We can't continue this way.

I don't pretend to know all the answers, and I'm well aware that alcoholism is a complex disease.

But I can tell you that we need to start questioning all of these stagnant beliefs and approaches.

If we continue to see alcoholism as a character failing, use incorrect and outdated medical terminology, and allow dangerous clichés to slip into our language, people will continue to die from it.

Babies will continue to be born with fetal alcohol syndrome, children will continue to be abused and neglected by alcoholic family members, drunk driving alcoholics will keep killing innocent people, relationships and lives will continue to be destroyed.

Let's used an evidence-based approach. It's good enough for every other disease.

I believe that a hundred years from now, just as we look back at the ridiculous medical notions and practices of people before us, future generations will look at ours and think how primitive we ever were for thinking about and treating addictions in the way we currently do.

What kind of culture sends people with an illness to a religion-based program that fails 90% of the time?

Ours does.

THE MEDICAL COMMUNITY

"It is highly disturbing that this drug is not made available to the patients that need it."[1]
—Dr. Heilig and Egli, 2006

When I started reading about this topic and realized that AA was not helping (and possibly even harming) most people who arrived at their doors with alcoholism, I felt angry at AAers.

But after a while I realized that people in AA are people with an illness who are just trying to keep themselves healthy and help others with the same illness to do so too.

They see people die around them and they cling, terrified, to the only life raft that someone has passed to them—whether it has a hole in it or not.

Their hearts are in the right place even if their methods are questionable and dangerous.

But people in AA come from the general population: usually it's not their job to look after the health of others.

But it *is* the medical community's job to look after others, by using evidence-based medicine as a guide for their decision-making.

It's their job to *do no harm*. But when it comes to alcoholism, they aren't doing a very good job.

It's a convenient and comfortable solution for doctors and others in the medical system to send people with addictions to free 12-step based programs.

It costs the system nothing, the doctor's time is not further 'wasted', and if the program fails to be effective, then the blame for its failure is always placed on the person with the addiction.

It's really the perfect business–if it doesn't work, it's not the *doctor's* fault now, is it?

The financial burden of subsequent illnesses as the alcoholic's health falls apart (triggering one or more of the 200+ diseases as mentioned earlier in the book) is never formally linked to the failure of the system to address the problem properly in the first place.

•••

I have a good friend who is a respected doctor.

When I first told her I was writing a book about pharmaceutical options for the treatment of alcohol dependence she laughed and asked me if my book was a work of fiction.

I'm not the first (nor will I be the last) to wonder why, (now that the facts and research are available–even to laypeople like myself), the medical community is not *leading* this approach to providing better treatment to people with alcoholism.

Doctors and other health care professionals can be wonderful, caring people. The good ones know how little they know; and that they can learn as much from their patients as from a textbook.

But developing a big ego is an occupational hazard for those in the medical profession.

Without enormous confidence, how else could you make life and death decisions?

And in our extremely hierarchical medical care system–where everyone knows the pecking order and there is no such thing as a flat structure–arrogance is encouraged and incubated.

Dr. Oliver Amiesen–a cardiologist, and the man who discovered the use of high-dose baclofen to treat his own alcoholism–wrote about the inability of his colleagues to admit flaws in their approach to treating alcoholics.

In his case, as he wrote, he:

> *"...spent countless hours via email and telephone answering questions about baclofen and advising people on how to speak to their physicians about it.*
>
> *In almost all cases, sadly, they could not convince their doctors to prescribe an unfamiliar medication off-label."*[22]

Amiesen blamed their ignorance on 'dogma'. He wrote that it "led me to wonder if people in addiction medicine and research might not be able to see beyond the dogma of their field—something that is common in every medical specialty, not to mention being a familiar fact of human nature."[22]

I looked up dogma. It means, "a belief or set of beliefs that is accepted by the members of a group without being questioned or doubted."' That sounds right.

There is another term I looked up.

Its definition is "a dereliction of professional duty or a failure to exercise an ordinary degree of professional skill or learning by one (as a physician) rendering professional services which result in injury, loss, or damage."

That's malpractice. And somehow that sounds right too.

EGO, DOGMA, AND STIGMA, OH MY

Is it ego? Is it dogma? Or is it something else: stigma.

There is another reason why medical professionals don't respond to alcohol dependence with medical skills.

And that is because many of them don't think addiction is a medical problem.

In one national study, US doctors were asked what proportion of alcoholism is a disease and what proportion is a personal weakness. The average proportion thought to be a personal weakness was 31%.

In another study of physicians, only 25 percent actually believed alcoholism to be a disease.[76]

In *Managing Alcoholism as a Disease*, the author wrote, "based on my experiences working in the addiction field for the past 10 years, I believe many, if not most, health care professionals still view alcohol addiction as a willpower or conduct problem."[77]

A survey of doctors at an annual conference of the International Doctors in Alcoholics Anonymous reported that 80 percent believe that alcoholism is merely bad behavior instead of a disease.[77]

In his 2014 JAMA article, researcher Edward Nunes suggested that to get medications more routinely utilized, doctors needed more training, but more importantly what is needed is "an embrace by all physicians, particularly those in primary care specialties, of the mandate to recognize and treat alcoholism and other addictions."[78]

Let me repeat that–he is simply asking doctors to "recognize and treat."

The 2012 report *Addiction Medicine: Closing the Gap Between Science & Practice* stated:

> "This profound gap between the science of addiction and current practice related to prevention and treatment is a result of decades of marginalizing addiction as a social problem rather than treating it as a medical condition."[3]

Compared with people suffering from other mental disorders that are not substance related[79] alcohol dependent people are much less frequently regarded as mentally ill, held much more responsible for their condition and their inability to change it themselves.[79]

In *The Deadly Stigma of Addiction*, Dr. Richard Juman writes:

"The idea that those with addictive disorders are weak, deserving of their fate and less worthy of care is so inextricably tied to our zeitgeist that it's impossible to separate addiction from shame and guilt.

Addiction comes with a second punch in the gut: the burden of being treated like a second-class citizen and expected to act accordingly."[80]

The definition of the word 'stigma' is "a mark of disgrace," and it is this black mark which clouds the lens through which the healthcare provider often views an alcoholic.

The Surgeon General has stated that stigma attached to mental illness constitutes the "primary barrier" to treatment and recovery.

Stigma is an insidious animal that only seems ridiculously out of place years after it has faded.

Years ago, long before breast cancer was pinkwashed, there was a great deal of stigma around it too. Its culture also contained a heavy element of shame and secrecy.

Some women weren't even told they had breast cancer. Others who were diagnosed with it kept it a secret or lied about what they had. Obituaries simply noted a 'long illness.'

At one time, even the New York Times refused an advertisement for a breast cancer support group.[81]

Today that sounds ridiculous. But stigma always looks that way in hindsight. It's like a retrospective stigma litmus test.

Dr. Juman says the "system is hard-wired to prolong stigmatization, and stigma contributes to addiction's lethality."[80] He gives several reasons why stigma in healthcare is lethal:

- People fail to seek treatment

- Medical professionals fail to treat addicts properly

- People with addiction are ostracized

- People in treatment are always under suspicion

- People in treatment are confronted with roadblocks constantly

- Stigmatization can contribute to poor treatment outcomes

That's all consistent with my experience.

For many people hearing about the state of alcoholism treatment, it reminds them of how depression was once treated and stigmatized.

Instead of diagnosing depression, doctors would describe patients with negatively charged terms like 'lazy' and 'slovenly.' Health care professionals looked at symptoms of depression through a warped moral lens.[79]

But a study that looked at changing perceptions over the last 10 years concluded that as more people came to understand the neurobiological underpinnings of mental illness, the more the social and moral judgments dropped.

Unfortunately, while that has helped destigmatize depression, the study showed that was not the case for alcoholism, where misconceptions were unchanged and the use of stigmatized labels actually grew by 16%.[82]

What changed for stigma around depression was that the medical community realized that medication could be used to treat it.

They started to prescribe early medications like Prozac and saw changes in their patients' functioning. And they realized that if a medication can be used to treat it, it might just be an illness, not a character defect after all.

One day that will be obvious for alcoholism too.

I'm not sure what it will take to get doctors to start doing their jobs.

But I hope that if enough patients bring enough research to enough doctors and make enough convincing arguments, that we'll nudge them into the 21st century for this disease too.

TREATMENT & THE REHAB INDUSTRY

"There simply is no other disease where appropriate medical treatment is not provided by the health care system and where patients instead must turn to a broad range of practitioners largely exempt from medical standards."[3]

— 2012 Report: Addiction Medicine: Closing the Gap Between Science & Practice

Before Amy Winehouse died of alcoholism she wrote a famous song about rehab and how she said "No, no, no."

It may have been a heartbreaking decision for her family. But had she spent a year in rehab, it may not have saved Amy anyways.

Families and loved ones of alcoholics will pin our hopes and dreams on anything when we see someone we love circling the drain. That, and the fact that the medical system is failing alcoholics, is what the private treatment industry feeds on.

A public system that fails consistently, plays right into the coffers of private care.

A critical 2012 report on medical treatment for those with addictions linked the emergence of an ineffective private treatment industry to the failures of a neglectful medical system:

"This neglect by the medical system has led to the creation of a separate and unrelated system of addiction care that struggles to treat the disease without the resources or the knowledge base to keep pace with science and medicine."[3]

Private addiction treatment is a money maker in the United States–a staggering $35 billion a year industry–and growing.[83]

It is also an industry that is mostly privately managed, not regulated by the government and run by unlicensed individuals where being 'in recovery' oneself is often the only line needed on a resume to justify an approach and become a treatment provider.

Marketing claims of fabricated success rates go unchallenged, and the families of sufferers become burdened with debt, remortgaging homes and maxing out credit cards to pay for expensive residential programs.

And of course, the basis of most private treatment is 12-step programs, which if offered by AA would be free, and which, as mentioned earlier, has no evidence of success anyway.[83]

If the treatments offered by most rehab centers don't work, though, why does the industry remain so profitable?

Here's why: Because there's nowhere else to turn.

When your loved one is staggering around on your front lawn as your children head off to school in the morning, what else is a loving family to do but *whatever they possibly can* to help their alcoholic.

And if helping that alcoholic means sending them away somewhere for 30 days to the only 'help' that is offered, so be it.

It may seem to be the only solution, and so families will send their alcoholics off to treatment until the bank won't lend them another dime, in the hope that 'one will take' or the alcoholic will finally 'smarten up'.

It's really the perfect business–if it doesn't work, it's not the *treatment center's* fault now, is it?

We watch these systems fail our loved ones.

It's agonizing and painful.

Some people survive.

A lot of them don't. It's born out in stories like this one:

> *"I lost my son to addiction and ultimately suicide.*
>
> *From the time I knew he had a problem until the day he died, I tried everything at my disposal to help him get quality care. He went to eight different programs and they all had a different approach; many offered conflicting advice …*
>
> *In the last weeks of his life, Brian was suffering from severe depression. On the day before he died, his aftercare program made the decision, without consulting Brian's therapist, or his parents, to terminate their relationship with him.*
>
> *At the time Brian most needed help, he was left alone.*
>
> *And so was I."*[3]

THE PHARMACEUTICAL INDUSTRY

There is an excellent article called '*Targeting Addiction*' that focusses on one scientist's (Dr. Bankole Johnson) groundbreaking research into the medication topiramate.[84]

The work–and the results–are impressive.

But not impressive enough for one comment-poster.

Shortly after the article was published, in 2010, a commenter using the handle 'Heisenberg' summed up his perspective on the 21-page article this way:

> "*It's all hogwash supplemented I'm sure by the drug companies.*"

His comment remains there today (as I write this book anyways). An ugly postscript to the last sentence of the article.

Aaaahh…. the Internet, where, in one dismissive sentence, anyone hiding behind a fake name can insult your integrity and your life's work, for all the world to see, pretty much permanently.

But the comment begs the question, was Heisenberg right?

While it's an easy and common conclusion to jump to if one distrusts big pharma, in this case, he couldn't have been farther from the truth.

In topiramate's defense, it is a medication with a wealth of data supporting its use in alcoholism treatment. (In other words–not hogwash).

But aside from that, topiramate (like the majority of medications that treat alcoholism) has several black marks against it which cause pharmaceutical companies to stay away.

First, there's a double whammy: Topiramate is both generic and off-label (as are many treatments for alcoholism).

So not only is there no money to be made for pharmaceutical companies in the marketing of topiramate, but they could face hefty fines if they did.

And next, all medications for addiction have an element that serves as a barrier to pharmaceutical company development and backing. And that is stigma.

Addiction medicine is a line of business that still carries with it a negative stigma that many in big pharma would prefer not be associated with.

And finally, up until recently, it's been difficult, if not impossible to be profitable with any medication that treats alcoholism. (Due to the AA effect described earlier).

None of these black marks—loss of marketing protection; off-label approval legislation; stigma or lack of profitability are realities that big pharma created. But they certainly do form a significant roadblock for them.

Before I go any further, in case Heisenberg wishes to come along and label my writing as pharma-supplemented hogwash, I'd just like to note—I am writing this entire book without any funding or endorsement from any company or organization—and that includes any pharmaceutical company.

Addiction may be an enormous market with vast potential, and pharmaceutical companies may be powerful money-hungry corporations on the look-out for the next Viagra. But medication for the treatment of alcoholism hasn't been good business for them so far.

Maybe Alkermes' strong profit announcement with Vivitrol will be just the signal that they need to begin to increase investment. But I suspect they will need to see some strong success with nalmefene in Europe, or another strong signal of change before a true turnaround begins.

And until that day comes, investments will remain small, researchers will continue to rely heavily on government funds and drug discoveries will fall consistently into the Valley of Death.

THE VALLEY OF DEATH

There is another factor that is compounding the lack of forward momentum in the further development of medications for alcoholism. And this is something that industry and government call 'The Valley of Death.'

(Is it just me, or is it strange that an industry that is so tied to human life and death uses a phrase like 'The Valley of Death', to describe a place where drugs go when the business case doesn't work out?)

The 'Valley of Death' is the black hole that medications can fall into between the point where a drug's potential is first discovered, and when a doctor uses that drug to treat a patient. Or to use an industry phrase—between the pathway from 'bench to bed'.

The vast majority of promising molecular discoveries by scientists fall into a couple of gaps in that valley, and never climb back out. Those gaps exist:

1) Between lab discovery and human clinical trial testing; and

2) Between human clinical testing and the doctor's office.

This valley exists for every area of medicine right now. It's a deep and growing chasm that industry leaders all over North America and Europe are struggling with.[85]

But because medications for alcoholism have not had a good track record of profitability, molecular discoveries that show promise for the treatment of alcohol addiction are far more likely to fall into that valley than medications that show promise for nearly any other major illness.

On one side of the divide are biomedical researchers and scientists who, at a cost of about $30 billion per year in the United States (NIH's budget for medical research), focus on understanding how diseases work and how they can be fought.

That's a relatively small feeder industry if you compare it to the other side of the valley where the health care system resides. It's a massive industry, with annual healthcare spending in the US costing over $3.8 trillion.

There used to be a system that bridged the gap between the two sides, but that bridge no longer works.

•••

In the fifties and sixties, medical research was often done by doctors.

Doctors were also scientists who spent time both in the lab and treating patients. There was no gap between discovery and treatment because doctors themselves bridged this gap.[85] Doctors didn't rely on pharmaceutical companies or the government to share medical knowledge with them to the same extent they do today.

Today, most research is done by highly specialized Ph.D. scientists.

So now, even if medications make it beyond the lab, most doctors don't learn about new discoveries.

And exacerbating the problem is the fact that the cost of getting a drug from discovery through to the end of clinical trials costs more and more every year. So pharmaceutical companies are that much more careful about which drugs they choose to shepherd through the process.

And then, once a drug is approved, even if research showed that the drug is useful for other illnesses, there are strict (million and billion dollar) fines applied to pharmaceutical companies that mention other applications for the drug in anything that can be construed as marketing.

So doctors never learn about other scientifically-backed uses for the medication.

Every single area of medical research is facing the same problem right now. Whether its cancer treatment, Alzheimer's or ALS, there are gaps in progress caused by the Valley of Death problem.

But medical research for people with addictions has more black marks to contend with than any area of medicine.

The lack of advancement in the medical community regarding addiction, the lack of support from AA, the stigma issue and no track record of profitability for alcohol addiction medicine means that no other area of medical research faces the same hurdles to drug development as this one. That's why the ones we already have–the ones that work–are truly precious.

PHARMA AND EXISTING MEDICATIONS

Earlier, topiramate was identified as having two issues that make it unattractive for pharmaceutical companies–it's generic, and off-label.

Generic medications that are on-label treatments for alcoholism (meaning they were FDA-approved specifically for alcoholism, not other illnesses), like naltrexone and acamprosate, are no longer protected by patent.

Any pharmaceutical company can make and sell them, and because generic medications are a commodity, there is much less profit in them, and drug companies usually discontinue marketing efforts around them.

Off-label drugs are those which have been found to be effective treatments for alcoholism, but were not officially approved for that medical treatment, like baclofen and gabapentin for example, which were approved for other medical purposes.

For off-label drugs, governments have put strict rules in place about pharmaceutical marketing, which bar pharmaceutical companies from marketing a drug for an off-label purpose.

Some pharmaceutical companies have received crippling fines for crossing the line.

In recent years for example, fines have been doled out in the billions for this practice: Johnson and Johnson ($1.391 billion), Glaxo Smith Kline ($1.043 billion), Pfizer ($2.3 billion) and Ely Lilly ($1.415 billion) all received massive fines for off-label marketing that would have bankrupt most companies.[86]

Topiramate was actually one of the drugs that resulted in a large fine for Ortho-McNeil Pharmaceutical and Ortho-McNeil-Janssen Pharmaceuticals, Inc. in 2010: both were fined for their role in promoting topiramate to psychiatrists for purposes it had not received approval for.

So why don't drug companies just take the off-label drug through the approval process so that it can be used for that purpose on-label?

Because it takes a lot of time and money to complete the studies and testing and other regulatory requirements involved in drug approval, and the drug would move closer to generic status each year that they invested in the approval process.

So, as highly respected addiction researcher Barbara Mason put it in a 2014 presentation about gabapentin, there is "no industry support for FDA approval of a new use for a generic drug that has shown promise for treating CNS (Central Nervous System) disorders," even ones with few other treatment options.[87]

The reality is that in the pipeline at the moment numerous drugs have shown initial signs that they may be helpful in the treatment of alcoholism. But very few of these are being developed for the treatment of alcoholism.

If they are in a drug company's development pipeline, with the exception of only a handful of medicines, they are being developed

(and could eventually be FDA-approved), for another purpose–
not for alcohol dependence. (So they would be off-label, and
unmarketable).

So the treatment of alcohol dependence with medication will
continue to rely predominantly on off-label drugs.

This means that the general public and medical system will likely
not learn about these medicines' ability to target alcoholism via any
communication channel funded by pharmaceutical companies.

This bears repeating: even when researchers prove that a drug can
help alcoholics; and even though that drug may have already been
proven safe in humans; it is unlikely to be supported or marketed
by a pharmaceutical company because of legislation that works
against it.

Gabapentin, and several others, for example, are safe, affordable,
readily available and effective.

They can save many lives. But they are not marketed and can't be
marketed for alcohol dependence.

DOES IT MATTER IF A PHARMACEUTICAL COMPANY DOESN'T MARKET A DRUG?

Does it matter if a pharmaceutical company can't market a drug?
Yes–very much so.

It's a sad fact of our system that it is extremely critical to patient
care whether a pharmaceutical company sees enough profit in a
medication to market it to doctors and patients. It doesn't seem
like our health should be dependent upon profit potential, but it is.

Many drugs are extremely well known and established, and for
those that have been incorporated into routine medical care, it
doesn't matter as much if the drug is no longer marketed to
doctors. Doctors are likely to be aware of it and prescribe it
anyways.

But if a medication is not well known either for its on-label or off-label capabilities, and it is not an established part of routine medical care (and nearly every important drug in this book falls into this zone), then it matters very much that a pharmaceutical company isn't marketing it.

Because your doctor is unlikely to hear about it and is therefore much less likely to prescribe it to you even if you bring it to their attention.

Medication that is marketed to doctors by pharmaceutical companies brings credibility. Medication that is marketed to doctors by patients is typically ignored.

While the pharmaceutical industry can be very heavily regulated by government healthcare arms, the government does not market medication.

The government instead relies on the business dynamics of the pharma industry to promote the medication that you and your doctor need to know about. But if this communication system that relies so heavily on pharmaceutical marketing breaks down in some way (as it has with medications for alcoholism), there is no 'plan b' that makes sure you get the right medications.

This peculiar weakness of the system leads pharmaceutical companies (at least those in health-care areas with profit potential) to do a ridiculously wasteful, time-consuming dance.

They look for ways around the system by developing variations ('biosimilars') of successful medications, which can be patented, win regulatory approval and which will then enjoy marketing protection.

In other words—they spend millions of dollars and decades of research, trying to discover drugs that have already been discovered.

SELINCRO LAUNCH IN EUROPE

With all of these barriers that pharmaceutical companies have experienced in developing medications for alcoholism, the nalmefene (Selincro) launch mentioned earlier in Europe is critical. It could change the entire face of alcohol addiction treatment.

Not only has Lundbeck launched a new product, but they are lobbying for approvals, endorsement and financial subsidization from influential governmental health groups across Europe; marketing to an army of doctors; and attempting to educate an entire health care system on hard-to-grasp concepts which includes two revolutionary 'new' concepts, which are:

(a) reduced drinking is just as important a goal as abstinence; and

(b) that alcoholism can be moderated, managed or even eliminated through medication.

It's an enormous challenge that they have taken on.

I have no affiliation with any pharmaceutical company, but I hope that Selincro sales go through the roof. I applaud Lundbeck, and CEO Ulf Wiinberg, for their work in improving conditions for people suffering from brain disorders, including addiction.

Lundbeck's 2015 Q2 report showed sales of DKK 51 M for the quarter and indicated that sales were being driven by the French market and showed "continued solid growth" in France, with slower growth in other areas.[88]

Nalmefene itself may not be a slam-dunk (the jury is still out), but the changes Lundbeck are introducing are critical. It's important that other pharmaceutical companies see that medication for the treatment of alcoholism can finally be effective *and* profitable.

STIGMA AND PHARMA IMAGE

Bell Canada is a Canadian telecom company that runs a campaign called 'Let's Talk'. Well-known athletes and celebrities are highlighted by the brand, speaking up about their struggles with mental health. It's a positive example of a major corporation leveraging its brand to help reduce stigma around mental illness. The company encourages Canadians to talk and text about mental illness.

This campaign contrasts heavily with the approach some pharmaceutical companies take. In a 2008 Newsweek article, Alan Leshner, the former head of the National Institute of Drug Abuse (NIDA) said, "companies with billion-dollar stakes in selling drugs for osteoporosis or cholesterol don't want their names on a product used by heroin addicts.[58]

Seven years later, the perception that ties addiction medication to the stigma attached to the people suffering from them seems not to have changed much.

In an informal review of the worlds' major pharmaceutical companies, very few of them (even those known to be investing funds and supporting research in the area), openly indicate addiction medicine as a research focus on their corporate websites. It's like addiction research is still a dirty little secret.

Profit potential can change all that, though.

Steven Paul, while he was the head of research at Eli Lilly, said there used to be a stigma attached to depression too, but Prozac put an end to it.

"Anything that has a large unmet need," says Paul, "is ultimately going to succeed commercially."[58]

DECLINE IN CNS INVESTMENT

There is yet another pharma industry issue hampering the development of new medications for alcohol addiction.

It's an issue which has professionals in all areas of mental health–not just addictions–worried. Development of CNS drugs (for Central Nervous System illnesses–of which alcoholism is one) is amongst the most expensive, highest risk area in medicine.

As pharmaceutical companies have come to realize the perils involved in CNS drug development, research and development in the field of mental health concerns has lost ground across the board.

One report, written by the Director of the US National Institute of Mental Health and Steven Hyman of Harvard University said that "Despite high prevalence and unmet medical need, major pharmaceutical companies are de-emphasizing or exiting psychiatry, thus removing significant capacity from efforts to discover new medicines."

The report pointed to the problems lying in "stringent regulations and approval processes for mental health drugs...as well as difficulty with developing medications that can be proven to actually combat mental illness."[89]

Since 2011, major companies Glaxo Smith Kline, AstraZeneca, and Novartis closed neuroscience divisions globally. And those significantly downsizing operations include Pfizer, Sanofi, Janssen and Merck.[90]

Pharma shareholders don't like to see companies they have invested in spend millions on new drugs only to have them fail before they make it to approval. There are only so many stock price drops senior executives will tolerate before the risk of further failure and loss leads them to reinvest in less risky areas of development.

The economics of neuropsychiatric drug development just aren't positive at the moment.

It takes 1.9 years on average to get regulatory approval (compared with an average of 1.2 years for all drugs). And human testing takes on average 8.1 years (two years longer than the average for all drugs). So counting the 6 to 10 years of preclinical research, drugs for CNS (Central Nervous System) illnesses take about 18 years to reach approval.[91]

When was the last time that you wanted to invest in anything that lost money for 18 years in a row before it had a chance to make a single dollar?

The harsh environment for CNS drugs means that only about 8.2 percent of those that begin human testing reach the marketplace, compared to 15 percent of drugs overall.[91]

CNS drugs are nearly twice as likely to fail as all drugs on average. And when CNS drugs fail, they fail at the most expensive, high-profile phase in the pipeline–in phase 3 trials. Only 46 percent succeed at this point (compared with 66 percent on average for all drugs).[91]

Recently, Pfizer, Johnson & Johnson, Eli Lilly and Baxter all experienced high profile failures in large phase 3 clinical trials for Alzheimer's while biotech Satori Pharma had to completely shut down operations after the poor performance of their Alzheimer's compound.[90]

If that's not a bleak picture of mental health drug development, I don't know what is.

And keep in mind that those numbers are for CNS drugs across the board–which include areas of intense interest such as Alzheimer's. The numbers are far more dismal for any drug related to addiction disorders.

A NEW WAY

However, companies with the stomach to stay in the CNS drug development game will benefit in some ways too.

If a company can develop drugs and remain profitable in the CNS drug development game, it's earned the chops to be profitable in any area of drug development.

These companies are developing new ways of doing business that the enterprises that exit the arena won't develop. And these new ways of doing business will serve the companies that learn them and help them in every area of development, giving them a competitive advantage against competitors who couldn't stomach or survive the risk.

The companies that are staying with CNS drug development are taking a hard look at how drugs have always been developed and changing things. In the past, drug development has been secretive, siloed and fraught with proprietary secrets. Information sharing across pharmaceutical companies was grounds for termination.

Now, there is much more innovation and collaboration. Instead of failing at enormous cost individually, competitors are minimizing risk and maximizing brain power by working together.

In an article in Scientific American called *A Dearth of New Meds*, the author writes that "ultimately, making new CNS medicines may depend on a networked approach to innovation, in which many organizations share in the risks and the rewards. It is clear that the challenges of developing new neuropsychiatric medicines are greater than any one company, institution or organization can bear alone."[91]

Pharmaceutical companies are working it out. Today, it is reported that the "vast majority of neuropharmaceutical development is being conducted in a partnership or collaboration basis. Most commonly, a smaller biotech's trials will receive 50-100% of the funding from one or more big pharma players, on conditions of key milestones being met."

This means that if trials flop, the big pharma partner can cut their losses, and a failure in a small partner's trial won't look as bad to shareholders as the same failure occurring from the company's own trial.[90]

Whereas once, small biotech players may not have had the resources to develop essential drugs, today the role they play in the CNS drug pipeline has become critical.

Companies like Merck, Roche, Glaxo Smith Kline and AstraZeneca are also investing in genetic research—a critical area since more and more mental illnesses have been shown to have a strong genetic biomarker component. (Alcohol dependence is no exception to this—many of the effective medications for alcoholism have been found to work best for individuals with very specific genetic markers and gene clusters).

By identifying genetic biomarkers, pharma can change how patients are selected for drug trials, significantly improving trial outcomes, perhaps even with previously failed drugs.

ADVANCEMENTS

There are exciting twinkles of hope for alcohol addiction medicine within small pockets of the pharmaceutical industry. And there are a few things that larger companies can take away from the firms that are making headway. Here are what some companies are doing in the area of alcohol addiction medication development.

RECKITT BENCKISER & INVIDIOR

Powerhouse Reckitt Benckiser is one of a handful of companies making strategic business moves in the space.

Its spin-off, Invidior, has been developing and marketing drugs for the treatment of opioid addiction for over ten years. In 2014, it made its first foray into a medication for alcohol addiction when it entered into a global licensing agreement with XenoPort Inc. to develop and market arbaclofen placarbil for the treatment of alcohol use disorder.

Invidior's CEO Shaun Thaxter says that arbaclofen placarbil is the company's biggest commercial opportunity and that they will be actively looking for opportunities to further expand their pipeline in the addiction arena.[92] Their press release stated that "there is a tremendous need for more effective, well-tolerated treatment options among the growing patient population with alcohol use disorders."[93]

The Invidior website is bold, forward thinking and has an inspiring message about addiction medicine which other pharma companies should take note of. It says:

> *"Our goal is to help remove the stigma of addiction, expand treatment access infrastructure, and to help patients take the first step in their journey—empowering them to act before the moment of readiness is gone.*
>
> *Together, we are making considerable progress in the U.S. and Australia, with the drug policy and regulatory environment moving towards recognizing addiction as a normal, legitimate disease, creating shifts in public perception, and allowing broader access to mainstream medical treatment models, similar to other chronic diseases.*
>
> *Globally, a movement is underway, with the EU also making strides to move away from a harm reduction environment towards a medicalized, recovery model like other chronic diseases.*
>
> *We intend to transform addiction from a global human crisis to a recognized and treated disease worldwide."[94]*

Is it marketing copy for shareholders? Sure. Did I drink the Koolaid? Yes, I did.

But it's also a step forward. Good on you Invidior.

ALKERMES

Alkermes may be the first pharmaceutical company in the alcohol dependence space that is seeing a substantial return on their investments–proving that profitability in this space is now possible–even with a new take on an old generic medication.

In July of 2015, Alkermes announced that they were improving the company's 2015 financial expectations driven by accelerating financial performance of Vivitrol, Alkermes' injectable naltrexone product for opiate and alcohol dependence.

Commented James Frates, Chief Financial Officer of Alkermes, "driven by the accelerating quarterly growth in net sales of Vivitrol, our long-acting injectable medication for the treatment of opioid dependence and alcohol dependence...net sales of Vivitrol were $37.2 million, compared to $21.6 million for the same period in the prior year, representing an increase of approximately 72%."[29]

But Vivitrol won't be a one-hit-wonder for Alkermes. They are translating their learnings and earnings from the naltrexone injectable into new treatments for alcohol dependence. They seem to have more compounds for the treatment of alcohol dependence in clinical trials right now than any other company.

Several compounds have performed well. Samidorphan, which has been reported to have similar efficacy to naltrexone but possibly with reduced side-effects[95], and ALKS-3831, an olanzapine/samidorphan combination targeted to patients with schizophrenia and alcohol use disorders both look promising.

A third CNS drug, ALKS-5461, recently failed to meet expectations in final studies, tanking the company's stock by an enormous 43%, and underlining the enormous risk involved in CNS drug development. But another Alkermes CNS drug, Aristada, was recently approved for treatment of schizophrenia.

Partnership and collaboration are a key strategy for Alkermes and they have successful partnerships with AstraZeneca, Janssen Pharmaceuticals, Acorda and Acceleron Pharma.

AstraZeneca

The AstraZeneca corporate website says, "The best science doesn't happen in isolation." And their extensive approach to partnering and collaboration has resulted in a few deals that hold promise. They have made strategic investments in two biotechs with promising addiction products (Eolas Therapeutics and Heptares).

Both have orexin-1 receptor antagonists in development which may be promising for addictions. They have also partnered with NIDA (National Institute of Drug Abuse) to explore Neuroscience iMed's (AstraZeneca branch) drug AZD8529, for smoking cessation. AZD8529 may also treat other substance abuse.[96]

And unlike so many pharmaceutical companies, they are not afraid to publicly mention addiction disorders[96] on their website as an area of focus.

They also have a core focus on personalized healthcare (medications driven and tested with the benefit of genetic research), and according to them, 80% of their programs benefit from this approach.

Lundbeck

Lundbeck is a crucial player in the alcohol dependence space right now, fighting on many fronts for Selincro's success in Europe and elsewhere.

In addition to their outstanding work with Selincro, Lundbeck is not afraid to stand up to mental health stigma.

In October 2015, Lundbeck celebrated World Mental Health Day, promoting dignity in mental health treatment. Their primary research and product focus is brain diseases, with alcohol dependence appearing prominently, listed first on their website.

OTHERS

Other inspiring work by other pharmaceuticals includes the following:

- Adial Pharmaceuticals (focused on addiction and founded by Dr. Bankole Johnson) is making steady progress with alcohol dependence medication AD04.[97]

- Addex Pharmaceutics' focus on collaboration with patient advocacy groups, academic institutions and governmental organizations including NIAAA (National Institute on Alcohol Abuse and Alcoholism) is paying off with progress for promising pre-clinical compounds as well as ADX71441.[98]

- XenoPort Pharmaceuticals is collaborating with the NIAAA in the development of their medication Horizant, as a potential treatment for AUD (Alcohol Use Disorder). The patent on Horizant (gabapentin encarbil) runs until at least 2026.[99] They've also been granted exclusive worldwide rights for the development and commercialization of carbaclofen placarbil, another promising medication.[100]

- Eolas is a specialty company committed to treating the disease of addiction. It recently signed a global licensing and partnership agreement with AstraZeneca for the development of a drug designed to block a neuropeptide associated with addiction to nicotine and stimulants such as cocaine, opiates, and alcohol.[101]

AstraZeneca's website states, "The collaboration is a great example of our unique approach to Neuroscience drug discovery and development, partnering to advance the most exciting scientific opportunities in areas of high unmet medical need."[96]

- Japan's Sosei Group Corporation purchased a smaller biotech–Heptares–in February 2015. Heptares has an orexin receptor antagonist in development which they hope will target the treatment of addiction and compulsive disorders.[102]

- France's D&A Pharma has several exciting projects to treat alcohol addiction in development. GHB has long been used in Europe effectively to help alcohol addictions but has several drawbacks, including its own addictive qualities. D&A Pharma have developed two variations on the drug–one is an immediate-release formulation which has been redesigned with lower abuse potential, and the second is an even more exciting variation, which has a longer duration of action.[103]

- Italy's Laboratorio Farmaceutico CT Srl has many years of experience in the study of new and innovative drugs for alcohol addiction. Laboratorio Farmaceutico initially developed the product Alcover (which is now being extended by D&A) and is currently developing a highly promising new medication called GET73 which is in the clinical study phase in the US.[104]

GOVERNMENT

Here's a story you may not have heard.

Barry's father moved back to the US in 1971, running away from a third broken marriage. Barry and his siblings knew his father could be a violent and abusive man, so the breakup of the marriage was no surprise.

His dad had no job and a car accident had left him severely injured. So he stayed with Barry for a short time in Hawaii to regroup, and then returned home.

At home, a second car crash cost him his legs and then a third one cost him his life.

As with the previous accidents, he had been drunk at the time, and behind the wheel.

Barry is—of course—Barack Obama, the President of the United States. And he knows something about alcoholism, because his father, Barack Obama Sr. was an alcoholic.

•••

In October 2015, President Obama, the Secretary of Health and Human Services, Sylvia Burwell, and the new czar, Michael Botticelli, spoke at a US town that had been hit hard by opioid addiction.

Between 2002 and 2013, heroin-related deaths in America nearly quadrupled. In 2013, 37,000 Americans died of drug overdose.

This shocking, hockey-stick shaped increase in overdose death is as good a visual depiction as any of the disaster that the war on drugs has turned out to be.

But there is a silver lining to this epidemic. It's the impetus for change that just might be needed to pave the way for a new approach to the treatment of addiction.

And that new approach will change the way alcoholics are treated too.

Because, after all, alcohol is a drug. Addictive drugs of abuse– whether cocaine, heroin, alcohol (or even, some might argue, tobacco)–all do the same thing–they hijack parts of brain. Some just kill more slowly than others.

The government's focus on MAT clears a path for all substance addictions. If MAT is supported, funded and legislated for one kind of substance addiction, it must be supported for all.

•••

Earlier in the book we covered some of the moves made by the Obama administration which will impact treatment made available to people with alcoholism.

There is a surprisingly long list of promising moves that the US government can be applauded for. They include:

- Appointing as a figurehead for this movement, a new Drug Czar who is a recovering alcoholic with strong ties to AA groups.

  The new Czar has publicly stated that "we have highly effective medications, when combined with other behavioral supports, that are the standard of care…[28]

- Introducing the term 'MAT' (Medication Assisted Treatment) into public vernacular; and publicly announcing support for this approach–and only this approach.[105]

- Taking the focus off of criminalization and onto medical treatment.[30]

  Obama has said, "rather than spending billions of dollars — taxpayer dollars — on long prison sentences for nonviolent drug offenders, we could save money and get better outcomes by getting treatment to those who need it."[30]

- Removing funding from judges who 'practice medicine from the bench' by removing federal funding from those courts barring addicts from receiving MAT.[28][106]

- Providing funding through the appropriations bill for medications like naltrexone and ensuring that substance abuse disorder is treated on par with other mental illness (which must be treated on par with other illness–period.)

  Obama has stated, "I've made this a priority for my administration ... And under the Affordable Care Act, more health plans have to cover substance abuse disorders. The budget that I sent Congress would invest in things like ... expanding medication assisted treatment programs."[30]

- Directing federal agencies with health care responsibilities 90 days to identify barriers to MAT and to come up with ways to remove them.[28]

•••

At the October 2015 event, the president and his team spoke about what they are doing to curb this overdose epidemic.

Burwell spoke about her top priorities. She said:

> *"Number one is changing prescribing practices...Second is working on medication assisted treatment."*

This is incredible news and such a promising announcement for proponents of MAT.

But let's step back for a moment and put this in perspective.

The drug overdose numbers sound bad–37,000 American deaths in 2013. But the number of people dying of drug overdose each year is *dwarfed* by the number of people that die in the US of alcoholism each year–88,000 people.[14]

And the epidemic of alcohol-related deaths has been going on much much longer.

But at the October event, alcoholism was not mentioned.

Given that it was an event focused on addiction, and as far as drugs go, it's alcohol–not opiates—that kills the biggest number of Americans, is there something wrong with this picture?

Yes.

But it's also a step forward.

Nobody seems to be screaming at the American government about all the dying alcoholics–so they aren't a priority.

And Obama, Botticelli and Burwell know that while an announcement by a political leader promoting medication for the treatment of alcoholism would not go over well, the 12-step movement was never as ingrained in the psyches of doctors and society for drug addiction as deeply as it was, and still is, for alcoholism.

It's easier politically–especially with the parents of many dead overdose victims in the audience from failed 12-step programs–for Obama to focus on tackling drug addiction with medication.

But while it may never be publicly stated, I would like to believe that for Obama and Burwell, MAT is as much about getting proper medical treatment for alcoholics as it is about getting medical care to opiate-users.

I believe this for two reasons.

First, you can see the names of medication for alcoholism beginning to show up in government directives that list medications for opiate dependence.

And second, just as it is for me, for Obama and Burwell, it's personal.

First–look at, as an example–one of SAMHSA's recent announcements:

> *"Recognizing that Medication-Assisted Treatment (MAT) may be an important part of a comprehensive treatment plan, SAMHSA Treatment Drug Court grantees are encouraged to use up to 20 percent of the annual grant award to pay for FDA-approved medications (e.g., methadone, injectable naltrexone, noninjectable naltrexone, disulfiram, acamprosate calcium, buprenorphine, etc.) when the client has no other source of funds to do so."*[106]

If there's any doubt that the government's new approach is strictly for opiate users, the list at the end of that order confirms otherwise.

Six drugs were mentioned in the announcement. Four of the six are treatments for alcoholism. And two of the six—disulfiram and acamprosate—are *exclusively* for the treatment of alcoholism.

There are no other addictions that those two medications are used to treat.

So if Obama's approach isn't just as much about alcoholism as it is about opiate overdose, those medications would never have made it into that list.

As for the 'it's personal' part, it's clear. As the earlier story showed, Obama had a father who died from alcoholism. The President was the child of an alcoholic and as such was deeply affected by this disease. Perhaps he struggles with it himself. Perhaps he worries that one of his children will inherit it.

And Botticelli (the Drug Czar) is of course the recovering alcoholic who endorses medication assisted treatment.

Both of them have seen and experienced enough heartbreak from alcoholism to know that if there is a medical solution, it needs to get to alcoholics—even if doing so involves some extremely strategic stepping.

LINCHPINS

"The linchpin sees the world very differently...The linchpin feels the fear, acknowledges it, then proceeds."
—Seth Godin[107]

The late artist François de Kresz drew a picture of a vast plain of sheep, all walking passively in the same direction together.

There's one little black sheep heading against the stream, politely saying 'excuse moi.... excuse moi... excuse moi...', as he heads away from the edge of a cliff–off of which the rest of the passive white beasts plummet.

That little black sheep is a linchpin–a term coined by author Seth Godin.

A linchpin is an ordinary person who does extraordinary things. Sometimes at great personal risk they defy the status quo and conformity. They head in their own direction, sometimes singularly; and their ideas and actions can create great change.

I've always admired linchpins, and in this story there are several. This chapter says thank-you to a few of them.

•••

At the time I wrote the original book, and as I write this one, there are no other books available that provide a single resource to alcoholics, their families or medical professionals that cover the range of available pharmaceutical options now available.

This resource–while much needed–just does not exist outside of my original book ('A Prescription for Alcoholics – Medications for Alcoholism')–either in book format or online.

Why governments of the world have funded billions of dollars in research to discover substances that help fight alcohol addiction, and then not spent a few thousand writing a book or building a website to let the general public know about them is a puzzle I don't have an answer for.

The discovery of research findings is important, but the translation of those findings into plain English is critical. Until scientific research is translated into plain English, it's lost on the majority of people that need it.

The majority of the information available on the topic of medications for alcoholism that is available in plain English was created not by science, medicine or government, but by a colorful collection of individuals–some highly credible in a traditional sense, and others unfortunately not.

To help others discover what they had already found, they published memoirs, personal case studies in medical journals, wrote Internet postings, launched websites, and crowd-funded a documentary.

And because of alcoholism's stigma and the AA effect, these people shared their discoveries at great cost to their careers, privacy, and reputations.

•••

The second 'A' in AA is not there by accident. Regardless of the danger some may present to those around them, maintaining anonymity for alcoholics and their families means that they don't fall further victim to stigma.

By maintaining anonymity, they avoid losing jobs and careers or facing lawsuits and the public humiliation and anger they would experience if they were outed.

Obama's Drug Czar Michael Botticelli himself said that it was much harder for him to come out as someone with an addiction, than as a gay man.

If you have not attended AA or one of the support groups, you may not realize who the people are around you that struggle with addiction.

There are alcoholics that teach grade three, while drinking gin from a coffee cup all day long; there are alcoholics who perform intricate surgeries, then binge themselves to oblivion on their days off; there are alcoholics who experience heavy withdrawal symptoms, as they drive massive 4-wheelers down the highway, there are alcoholics sipping from a hidden mickey before clocking in for their shifts in the nuclear power plant up the street. You've met them, I've met them.

Sadly, alcoholism is a disease that can cause great harm to those without it.

For an alcoholic to stand up and speak about their alcoholism and argue for the use of medication in treatment, they must be comfortable in outing themselves and their loved ones and transforming their private desperation into a public affair.

So when anyone steps forward and publicly declares themselves an alcoholic to advocate for other medical options, they are often putting their careers, licenses, and lives in jeopardy in ways we might not immediately see.

Even non-alcoholics–doctors and writers like Gabrielle Glaser for example–who stand up against the status quo, are exposing themselves to threat.

Sharing information without the shield of anonymity, discussing their own alcoholism publicly, sharing non-conventional medical approaches, or standing up under harsh public scrutiny from the public and the powerful AA and rehab groups is not without significant risk.

Despite this, a handful of people have gone public and shared information without the security of anonymity.

Among others, these pioneering individuals include:

- The late Dr. Olivier Amiesen, a French-American cardiologist who died of a heart attack in 2013 after publishing a book and series of medical articles on the medical cure he discovered for his own severe alcoholism;

- The late Dr. David Sinclair, a quirky American neuroscientist who made his home in Helsinki and was the grandfather of addiction research in 'as needed' methods of treatment.

Other notable linchpins, some of whom I'll tell you more about, include Claudia Christian, Dr. Roy Eskapa, Dr. Fred Levin, the late R. Evan Picard, Dr. Linda Garcia and Dr. Phillip E. Thomas.

DOCTORS, WRITERS & ALCOHOLICS

DR. OLIVIER AMEISEN

When I think of the handful of people who have risked their careers to help alcoholics find medical treatment, the face that always immediately comes to mind is that of French-American cardiologist Dr. Olivier Ameisen, posing for a May 2010 article in *The Guardian* about his work in the field.

In the photo, at the age of 56, Ameisen looked tired and gaunt, but determined. Written on his face perhaps one can read the years of work and study that put him at the top of his field; the debilitating anxiety he medicated with alcohol; the years spent struggling with severe alcoholism, and the effort of the fight he began once he cured his own alcoholism with baclofen, to let others in the medical community know of his discovery.

Sadly Dr. Ameisen died on July 18, 2013, but during the final decade of his life he left an incredible legacy. This cardiologist and symphony-level pianist did more to advance the treatment of alcoholism with medication in a single decade than most addiction physicians do in their lifetimes.

In the late 90s and early 2000s, desperate to find a medication to treat his own severe, debilitating alcoholism, Amiesen never gave up trying treatments and medications. After tireless research and self-experimentation, he finally treated himself with high doses of baclofen. One day, amazingly, he realized that he was "completely and effortlessly indifferent" to alcohol.[22]

Knowing that his discovery could save the lives of thousands of other alcoholics, Amiesen spent the rest of his life trying to get the medical community to take notice.

Publicly 'outing' himself as an alcoholic, he bravely wrote his experience as a 'self-case report.' It was published in December 2004 in the journal Alcohol and Alcoholism, published by the Oxford University Press.

As Amiesen wrote in his excellent 2008 book, 'The End of My Addiction':

> *"A deafening silence ensued. Except for Giovanni Addolorato and a few of his colleagues in Italy, no one inside or outside the field of addiction research and treatment seemed to have any interest in the first peer-reviewed report of complete suppression of the deadly disease of alcoholism with the alleviation of comorbid anxiety."*[22]

And in the entire year after the paper was published, only two people in the medical and research community contacted him.

Because of Amiesen's journal publication, the subsequent publication of his book (which circumvented the dogmatic medical community and was written for those suffering from alcoholism and their families) and his tireless work until his untimely death, Amiesen helped thousands of people find a way out of alcoholism.

After reading Ameisen's book, another doctor–Dr. Phillip E. Thomas began to take baclofen himself, completely suppressing his own cravings for alcohol and allowing him to have an occasional drink in a social setting.

Inspired by Amiesen's bravery, Thomas also bravely published his own self-case report in the journal *Progress in Neurology and Psychiatry*.[108]

Due to Ameisen's efforts, in June 2014, the French government became the first government to recognize the importance of baclofen in the treatment of alcoholism by publicly announcing that it would reimburse patients for the cost of baclofen when used in connection with the treatment of alcoholism.

In the United States, what Ameisen accomplished would be the equivalent of gaining both FDA approval *and* public health care insurance reimbursement for the treatment of alcoholism with baclofen–something unlikely to happen for many years.

FATHER OF ADDICTION RESEARCH DR. DAVID SINCLAIR

Dr. David Sinclair was a kindly and quirky American-born research scientist who spent much of his life's work in Finland, focused on addiction medicine.

His contributions to the field were groundbreaking and extremely relevant even today. Thousands of people whose lives have been saved by naltrexone and the 'as needed' method developed by Sinclair can credit him with saving their lives.

Sinclair passed away in April 2015. And at the end of his obituary, it states, "In honor of David's life, his family requests that you learn about The Sinclair Method of alcohol treatment and then help others become educated about it."[109]

Despite his impactful work, recognition of Sinclair's contributions (aside from the many citations and references to his research publications in science and medical journals) seems strangely absent in North America.

Perhaps because Sinclair's discoveries and hypothesis' were so far ahead of his time, the world of addiction research and medicine looked at him more like an outlier than as the innovator he has proven to be.

There are only a few medications that have gained FDA-approval or European medical approval specifically for their use in alcoholism (others are effective for alcoholism, but have gained their FDA approval for the treatment of other, non-related illnesses).

In Europe, one of a handful of drugs specifically approved for the treatment of alcoholism is nalmefene, which is currently patented and marketed by Lundbeck[110][111]. However, it was Dr. Sinclair who first patented nalmefene[112] in 1992.

And in the United States and Canada, one of the few FDA-approved (and Health Canada approved) medications is naltrexone, which also was first patented by Dr. Sinclair,[113] in 1989.

Sinclair also demonstrated and conducted very early research into the Alcohol Deprivation Effect (ADE), which is the addiction/detox/binge behavior seen in lab rats and which has been researched and observed by other scientists many times since.

Very early on, Sinclair also wrote extensively about the Pharmacological Extinction Hypothesis, which is a now often-cited theory used to explain the effectiveness of naltrexone and nalmefene when taken by alcoholics as needed.

Based on his understanding of alcoholism and naltrexone, Sinclair developed a method of taking naltrexone–the 'as needed' method, which was coined TSM–or The Sinclair Method.

In 2012, Dr. Roy Eskapa, a clinical psychologist who had worked with Dr. Sinclair wrote a book (with a foreword written by Dr. Sinclair) about treatment with naltrexone using TSM.

The book, ('*The Cure for Alcoholism: The Medically Proven Way to Eliminate Alcohol Addiction*') is an excellent resource and defacto 'how to guide' for taking naltrexone in the manner that Sinclair developed. (Though if naltrexone does not turn out to be the cure for you–remember there are many other effective medications available).

ACTRESS AND ADVOCATE CLAUDIA CHRISTIAN

Claudia Christian is a beautiful American actress who may be best known for her starring role in the 90s sci-fi hit Babylon 5, creating a cult-following with the Comic-Con crowd.

In the late 90's late-onset alcoholism began to wrap its tendrils around Christian. She started drinking too much, too often, binging and detoxing her way into addiction and desperation.

One day, in a detox center she came across a pamphlet on the monthly naltrexone injection, Vivitrol. The pamphlet led her to research naltrexone and come across the book written by Dr. Roy Eskapa based on addiction research pioneer Dr. David Sinclair's method for taking naltrexone.

Just as Baclofen had worked astonishingly well for Dr. Olivier, Christian was one of the lucky ones when it came to naltrexone. She wrote about her amazing recovering from alcoholism in her excellent 2012 book *Babylon Confidential–A Memoir of Love, Sex, and Addiction*.[114]

Christian became heavily committed to helping other alcoholics recover using naltrexone as she did. She started an organization (cthreefoundation.org) and released an outstanding documentary she produced and appeared in called '*One Little Pill.*'

The documentary provides excellent insight into naltrexone for alcoholism. (Though abstinent individuals who are very reactive to alcohol imagery cues may wish to avoid watching the documentary as it could trigger intense cravings.)

Still a working actress (recently appearing in the Mentalist, Castle, and Criminal Minds), Christian is one of the dominant forces that have allowed naltrexone to become more widely known, saving many lives.

And despite her fame, Christian still works at a grass-roots level. I'll always be grateful to Christian: once when I was still very early in learning about alcoholism medications, she reached out privately by email to me, encouraging me to continue my work.

COURAGEOUS DR. FRED LEVIN & THE LATE R. EVAN PICARD

One of the most difficult barriers for alcoholics to overcome is simply to find a doctor who will prescribe medication like baclofen and naltrexone to them and who will support them in their treatment.

However there are individual doctors who, after prescribing medication successfully to some of their patients, realized the desperate need for doctors who would write the right prescriptions and support the medical treatment of alcoholics.

After treating 40 patients successfully with baclofen and following Dr. Amiesen's work closely, Dr. Fred Levin made it known online that he was willing to advise those who would otherwise treat themselves, over the phone, out of hours, so that they could take Baclofen safely with medical support.

Levin helped hundreds of alcoholics who couldn't find help elsewhere to obtain both medication and medical supervision.

Baclofen is a safe, FDA-approved medication. But if someone discontinues the drug suddenly it can result in serious depression. Levin not only gave alcoholics access to baclofen, but he provided them with the medical support to ensure that they took it (or reduced from it) safely.

In August 2013, Levin, who was an associate professor in the department of psychiatry at Northwestern University Feinberg School of Medicine, and at the Chicago Institute for Psychoanalysis where he taught neuro psychoanalysis for 10 years, was sanctioned by the state of Illinois.

He was charged by the Illinois medical board with "unprofessional conduct, improper prescribing of controlled substances and failure to establish and maintain medical records."

The respected physician, 71-years old at the time, was fined $10,000 and his license was placed on probation indefinitely.

The message boards used by so many of the people that Levin had helped lit up. Individuals whose lives Levin had saved defended him.

One individual—the late Evan Picard (known as Lo0p—whose life Levin had saved, and who had gone on to help hundreds more find help with baclofen), broke his anonymity to start a letter writing campaign. Many of the comments published on the board speak for themselves.

•••

This is all just so, so, so sad.

He sacrificed his career for us. He didn't ask for much money…he believed so strongly in the medication that he was willing to go out on a limb to help alcoholics. He was so kind. I know that what he was doing was legally questionable, but he was a believer. I give him full credit for saving my life back in late 2010 when I was hopeless and lost. I am so sad he can't continue helping more lost souls who need his help.

•••

I'd be honored to write a letter for Dr. Levin. He believed in me when I was lost and almost beyond hope. He helped me find my way out. I'm forever grateful.

•••

Dr. Levin has selflessly provided his services to myself and other alcoholics like me, asking virtually nothing in return. Several times, I found myself asking him about compensating him for his services because he never even billed me for it. It seemed as if he was doing it, simply to be of service and help those in need.

He also made himself available via phone, at ANY time, if I needed to discuss my treatment or had any questions, concerns or problems. Dr. Levin is anything but a "mail-order Doc", who is just shelling out prescriptions to anyone with a checkbook.

•••

I humbly ask that you please reinstate his medical license and allow him to continue his invaluable treatment to me and many others who have been freed from the hells of alcoholism. Without his care, I will be forced to stop taking baclofen and return to a life of alcoholic misery.

He is a passionate and caring doctor who dedicated himself to helping those in need and should not be punished for it.

I was destitute when I approached him. He said: "If you can send me a check for $10, do that."

So I did. He filled my baclofen prescriptions for 2 years, for $10. He also made himself available to me whenever I needed him. For $10.

•••

It was Dr. Levin who had the courage back in 2011 to prescribe baclofen for my son when he really needed it...and it made all the difference. It broke the cycle of anxiety and craving and gave my son space to get his life back together. I will be forever grateful.

Dr. Fred Levin prescribed baclofen off-label to alcoholics nationwide at a reasonable cost. He has saved the lives of hundreds as a result. Countless others have benefited from knowing he was there as a resource, and from his emerging prominence as an advocate for baclofen, an FDA-approved medication.

OUTSPOKEN AUTHORS

In addition to the alcoholics, doctors and researchers I've cited here, several authors stand out for their controversial and outspoken work criticizing the AA approach extensively.

They include:

- Dr. Lance Dodes, author of '*The Sober Truth: Debunking the Bad Science Behind 12-Step Programs and the Rehab Industry.*'[61]

- Gabrielle Glasser, author of both '*Her Best-Kept Secret: Why Women Drink-And How They Can Regain Control*'[115] and more recently a scathing but on-the-mark article for *The Atlantic* entitled, '*The Irrationality of Alcoholics Anonymous*'.[15]

- Dr. Peter Ferentzy, outspoken author of '*Dealing with Addiction: Why the 20th Century was Wrong.*'[11]

- Terrance Hodgins, the author of *The Orange Papers*, an extensive collection of essays that will make you rethink AA, found at orange-papers.org.

- Roberta Jewel & Dr. Linda Garcia, authors of the first self-account of recovery from alcoholism using topiramate. The book ('*My Way Out…*', spawned a forum on the mywayout.org website that is a lifeline for many alcoholics looking for an alternative to AA.

- Kenneth Anderson, author and advocate for evidence-based strategies. He founded the HAMS Harm Reduction Network (hamsnetwork.org) and published '*How to Change your Drinking*' in 2010 that provides treatment alternatives to AA.

THE ANONYMOUS

There are many hundreds of people who quietly and anonymously help alcoholics and their families discover medical options for the treatment of alcoholism.

They are active on forums—encouraging, cheering on successes, translating research and helping pick up the pieces when things don't go well.

I invite you to meet them by reading through the forum sites I have mentioned in this book (thesinclairmethod.net or mywayout.org/forum are two examples).

RESEARCHERS

"If I have seen a little further it is by standing on the shoulders of Giants."
Isaac Newton

In my research I have read the work of doctors, researchers, and scientists who have spent their lives seeking funding in a severely under-funded space, conducting research and slogging away in the trenches of science to further addiction medicine.

For every one of the hundreds of research reports I read, these scientists and others spent thousands and thousands of thankless hours working meticulously in offices and basement labs.

I imagine that one might start to seriously question their life's work and career choices in the middle of the night in an empty lab surrounded by drunken rats. But these are scientists who stuck with their research nonetheless.

I wanted to list some of them, but I realized that for every one that I list I'll probably be excluding five more that should be listed too. However many of their names appear throughout the book, as well as in the bibliography at the end.

For all the poignant and touching real life stories of alcoholics whose lives were saved by the medications written about in this book, these are the men and women that saved those lives.

06 | THE BOTTOM LINE

"In homes, doctors' offices, hospitals, schools, prisons, jails and communities across America, misperceptions about addiction are undermining medical care.

Although advances in neuroscience, brain imaging and behavioral research clearly show that addiction is a complex brain disease, today the disease of addiction is still often misunderstood as a moral failing, a lack of willpower, a subject of shame and disgust."

–Dr. Drew E. Altman, CASA Columbia National Advisory Commission on Addiction Treatment

Prescribing Practices Must
Change

Fundamentally, (naively?), I believe that the number one thing that has to change is how doctors treat alcoholics.

Regardless of all of the issues around AA, the treatment industry and the pharmaceutical industry, the one group that can change this entire picture are doctors.

When doctors start treating patients with evidence-based care for their alcohol addictions, other stakeholders will fall in line, or simply get walked over.

If more doctors prescribe evidence-based treatments, more people suffering from alcohol dependence will regain control and begin to lead happy healthy lives again.

Others will see these changes and request medications from doctors, which will reinforce evidence-based prescribing habits.

As happened with other heavily stigmatized mental illnesses like depression, as people see that alcoholism can be treated medically, it will become more widely understood that it is a disease, and less stigmatized.

Doctors will seek information and solutions from pharmaceutical reps, and pharmaceutical companies will be financially-motivated to further market medications and fund research into new medication.

Researchers will be motivated to continue researching and will be better supported by government and big pharma.

Treatment centers will start, as they already have, to incorporate evidence-based treatment into their programs, as a matter of survival.

Is this a pretty and naïve picture I am painting? No. All of this is starting to happen on a small scale already.

This book is a little cog in the wheel of that larger change.

So doctors, please—the lives of so many people with alcoholism depend on you.

- Read the scientific studies referred to in Volume 4 (or the original book—'A Prescription for Alcoholics – Medications for Alcoholism') with an open mind.

- Read the free study—'*Addiction Medicine: Closing the Gap Between Science and Practice*'[3] It's thorough, free, on the mark and with many recommendations on how to change the way we do things. Google it or find a link to it on www.aprescriptionforalcoholics.com

- Start integrating Medication Assisted Treatment and evidence-based practices into your work.

•••

And for the rest of us:

Write a letter.

Have a conversation.

File a complaint.

Give this book to someone.

Set up a meeting with a doctor.

Build a website.

Share your story.

CHAPTER SEVEN

07 | BEARING WITNESS

RANDY'S STORY

Some people believe there are no coincidences or accidents. That things unfold as they always were meant to unfold.

Logic tells me that's nonsense. But there's another little voice that tells me otherwise.

The little voice says that I was meant to meet Randy, meant to watch him struggle, be his friend, research all this stuff, write this book, lose him.

The little voice says maybe *you* were meant to read this book.

Maybe this book was intended *just* for you—someone I have never met. And maybe what you do next is one more link in a chain of events that are unfolding just as they were intended to.

•••

When we bear witness, we tell the stories that are too big, too profound to keep inside anymore.

Sometimes, by telling someone's story, we are saying, "This is what happened. It shouldn't have been this way. Let's not do this to anyone *ever again.*"

I think this whole book is my way of sharing that sentiment. So here's Randy's story.

•••

I'm going to tell you some stories about Randy. But before I do, I hope you can keep this picture of him in your mind:

Randy was a guy who once had a beautiful wife (his high school sweetheart), a young son, a lovely house, a hockey team he played on, a boat on his driveway, a group of good friends, a close family, vacations in the Caribbean, and a white- collar job he excelled at.

He was good natured, funny and good looking. He lit up a room with his smile. He was gifted with anything mechanical, could excel at any sport, and was a born entertainer. He was the life of the campfire, singing songs and entertaining with his guitar.

Growing up, he was a good kid. He stayed out of trouble. He followed rules, went to college, didn't pick fights. He spent summer weekends on the beach with his family looking for someone to take him waterskiing.

He was an extremely *normal* guy. And in so many things he was blessed.

If there was a picture next to the phrase 'wasted potential' in the dictionary, it would be his. And he knew it. He told me that once.

It was like a cruel twist of fate gave him all these gifts, and then gave him a disease that wasted all of them.

Randy was on a train. People joined him and sat with him on the journey sometimes. Some for longer than others. Eventually the train went faster and faster. We all got off one by one and then watched him as the train went out of control, crashed and burned. Nobody could stop it, not even him.

I've heard people explain his alcoholism by saying, "He had 'deep seated' issues," or 'demons'. I think I probably knew him better than anyone did, in his last few years anyway. And I don't think that demons or issues were behind his alcoholism.

When sober, which he was the majority of the time, he was happier and more mentally balanced than just about anyone I knew.

I believe he simply had a disease in his brain, deeply rooted in his DNA, passed to him from his father, called alcoholism.

I hope that as you read, you'll remember how I just described him. Because you won't see the happy, healthy, blessed Randy in my stories.

And if you find yourself starting to judge, please remember that what happened to him could happen to anyone—even you.

•••

One of the stories that I remember vividly is this one. It's not the worst story, but for some reason it stays with me, it symbolizes something–maybe powerlessness.

Once, after being sober for a few months, Randy saved up his money and purchased a used bike.

It was a big expense for him–he rarely spent money on himself when sober.

When Randy loved something (whether it was a cup of coffee, or a cat), he loved it enthusiastically and emphatically.

And he loved this bike like that. Probably in the same way that a kid on a bike feels freedom for the first time, Randy felt free when he rode that bike.

A few weeks after he bought it, he relapsed.

When Randy was drinking it was very common for him to drink and drive, but he had seen police in his area, so instead of driving, he rode the bike to the liquor store instead.

He was a week or two into the binge when this happened, so he probably looked like a mess–with stained clothes and a scruffy face.

Leaving the liquor store, he had two bags full of bottles–one on each arm. But between the effect of intoxication and the weight and awkwardness of the bags, he was having trouble riding his bike, wobbling around, zigzagging.

Over 6 feet tall, he lost control, flew off the bike, hit the ground hard and just missed landing on his own smashed bottles.

As he said to me later, he just picked himself up, turned around and rode back to the store.

He was afraid the store would close and he'd have no alcohol all night. That was a scary thought, and so he bought more to replace the smashed bottles, and once again rode off on his bike.

He soon realized that he was having just as much trouble as the first time. He fell off again.

This time, he gave up on the bike and dropped it on the lawn of a house he had been passing by.

He didn't lock the bike and didn't go back to get it. He had to get home to drink.

By the time he had sobered up again, a week or two later, of course the bike was long gone.

We cruised slowly past the spot at the side of the busy road where he had abandoned it, and it was such a sad, puzzled look he gave to the patch of lawn where he'd left it.

That was life for Randy though.

It was just one more regret piled on hundreds of others that were part of living with alcoholism.

And the lost bike was really just one of the little ones.

The ones that weighed most heavily on him were the regrets he felt about losing precious time and connection with his son, disappointing his family, and hurting people he loved.

•••

A few months after I met him, I found out he was a binge drinker.

He would follow his urge to drink at any cost.

He would start drinking and then be unable to stop. He would drink eighteen hours a day, non-stop for weeks at a time. If you have ever seen someone drink like this, you'll know, without a shadow of a doubt, that there is something wrong with them.

I never had a single doubt in my mind that alcoholism was a biological disease–a major malfunction of some system in the body–after I saw this.

He didn't enjoy this. It made him sad, lonely, depressed and sick. He couldn't really explain why he did it, but it was like he was a prisoner to it.

When I first came across him during one of these binges, I had never seen anything like it.

He sat in a dark basement surrounded by hundreds of cans and bottles, piles of partially eaten take-out food, wrappers and garbage. It was unfathomable that one person could drink so much. When alcoholism took hold of Randy, he was obsessed with and driven by alcohol over all else.

The room stank and he stank. It was disgusting. He looked at me, ashamed. Spills and carpet stains dried around him. He wore stained clothes he hadn't changed in days, he had grown a beard, his face was puffy and bloated. He reeked of vomit and alcohol.

It's not a pretty picture and I guess I could keep it to myself. But there is too much secretiveness and shame in alcoholism already. This is what the disease looks like behind the closed doors of many homes—maybe yours.

I came to learn that he had destroyed his very successful sales career, most of his family refused any contact with him, he had few friends, he had been bankrupt, and he owned nothing but his Ford F10. Eventually, during the time I knew him, he was evicted four times and became a regular visitor to the food bank.

He'd been in and out of rehab programs, treatment programs and Alcoholics Anonymous for years.

On a scale of 1-10, where 10 is a seriously ill alcoholic, I would give him a 12.

•••

On several occasions, I tried to help Randy access medical services he needed.

We met very kind people in the healthcare system from time to time. People who seemed to understand, saw him as a human, and truly seemed to care.

But every now and then during these times I observed the failure of a few others in the helping professions to treat him with respect and dignity.

The sudden discontinuation of alcohol in one's system can send your brain into a state of anxiety that most of us have only ever felt momentarily if we've lost a child at the fair, or discover we've left our wedding ring in a public bathroom.

And it was during times when his brain was going into anxiety overdrive, as alcohol left his system—that Randy would sometimes experience this disregard from the healthcare profession.

Sadly, there is a different set of care standards for people with addictions.

Once, I spent a day with him when he wanted to stop a binge and was seeking help from a public detox facility.

Some detox facilities seem to want people visiting them to feel like naughty children. They sometimes seem like detention centers, not places where sick people seek help. At this particular one, even if the people seeking help had checked themselves in freely (as Randy did), no cell phones or computers were allowed at any time. If they left they weren't allowed back. They were grouped together in rooms on cots just feet away from one another.

When people die of Alcohol Withdrawal Syndrome (AWS), one of the main reasons is because of the complications of seizures they can experience.[116]

Any alcoholic experiencing AWS, who has had a seizure during detoxification (as Randy had), needs medication to protect them from the further possibility of a deadly seizure.

The detox place we went to, despite being associated with a hospital, and despite being full of people who needed medical help, had no medical staff. And they wouldn't let him in without the seizure medication he needed.

As he had stopped drinking before our drive there, by the time we tried to register at the center, he started experiencing alcohol withdrawal syndrome.

It was Sunday, and so we headed to a hospital emergency room to get the needed prescription. As he vomited and shook, we were sent to the back of the line. People who were 'really sick' came in, waited their turn, were checked out and left while we sat there waiting.

Five hours later we gave up, and taking the letter the detox facility had given us (on their hospital letterhead, specifying the necessary medication), we drove to a walk-in clinic.

After waiting another hour to see him, the doctor dismissively said no to the prescription.

I pointed the letter out to him once more.

He said no.

I told him I would escort Randy straight back to the facility where the staff would store the medication. I asked him to call the detox facility to verify the letter.

He said no.

I told him I wouldn't leave his office until he called the facility.

He finally called them.

He was terse with them on the phone, hung up on them, and then again said no. I had no patience left. It took everything I had not to whack a row of clinic brochures off the counter as we left.

Randy was quiet and placid through the whole exchange. I was new to this treatment, but he was used to it. It had been drilled into him that he was to blame; that he'd brought it on himself.

We drove back to the emergency room and four hours of shaking and vomiting later finally met a very kind doctor who gave us the prescription. He seemed to be one of the rare few that understood.

I puzzled later over this experience. Had I not been there with my car to drive him from facility to facility, and with money to pay for the prescription, he would not have been able to access the detox facility himself.

I started to understand why, even when alcoholics reach out for help (something which can be difficult to begin with), it seems so difficult to obtain it.

Of course (as I knew would happen), later AA friends scolded me for enabling him. They said "Randy is a big boy" and that I should not have helped in the first place. "He's taking advantage of you," they said.

Maybe you agree with them. Many people would.

But perhaps try re-reading those paragraphs again, and this time remove Randy from the picture.

Replace him with your beloved (non-alcoholic) spouse, or child or friend.

Imagine you are trying to access medical care so that they do not have a seizure and die while trying to access further care.

In that scenario, would that experience–the delays and refusal of treatment for your loved one–someone who is ill and at serious risk of a seizure that could result in permanent brain damage– would that be okay with you? Or would it infuriate you?

Does it represent a good standard of care in a first world country?

Did your perception of whether the experience was okay or not change when you took the alcoholic out of the picture?

If it did, then that may be a measure of your own stigma. We all start off with it. We are all a product of the same societal influences.

•••

When Randy relapsed, his family and friends were always angry, disappointed, worried, and afraid for him. He knew his mother woke up in the middle of the night with her heart racing, terrified for his safety. His father was furious at him for what he 'did to his mother', and wouldn't talk to him for months afterward.

He didn't want to hurt anyone—didn't want to do this to them. But each time he relapsed, he did it again.

He said to me, sobbing, frustrated, feeling the weight of letting his family down, "my god, I try, please, tell them how hard I have tried."

And I agree with him—Randy tried *so hard* not to be an alcoholic.

I truly never saw anyone try so hard to change in my life.

I think some around him would disagree with me. Friends told me angrily, that before I knew him, he would always leave any kind of treatment program early.

And now that I know what I know about 12-step programs and treatment centers, and how they don't really help at all, I don't blame him for leaving early.

He was genetically hard-wired for alcoholism.

I'm sure he was well aware that treatment was doing nothing for him.

•••

When Randy relapsed, as he consistently did, this is what it was like.

He would drink until he had spent every dollar he had. His credit card would be maxed out and his bank account emptied.

Then he'd pawn anything he owned to buy alcohol. His apartment would be bare—left with no possessions—no TV, no laptop, no cellphone.

When he came out of the 2-3 week binge, he would have to pick up the pieces of his life.

Two hours after his last drink, he would start to go through physical withdrawal.

He would experience severe anxiety, shakiness, weakness, be hot one minute and freezing cold the next.

His throat would be raw and swollen from so much alcohol, but through it he would vomit and dry heave.

A few times during withdrawal he had a seizure.

He'd be weak, exhausted, with stomach problems, insomnia and wasted muscles. He never complained about this though. He always felt he deserved it.

But emotionally, things would be much worse.

He would have to deal with the embarrassment of his drunken behavior (lies, missed fathers' days, missed visits with his son, missed work, missed payments) and the relationship carnage that he had created during the binge—angry friends, angry family, angry customers, angry everyone.

Deeply ashamed, he'd face all these people, including his AA sponsor, who was inevitably frustrated and disappointed in him and threatening to no longer sponsor him.

As is AA's practice, he would face his actions and make amends to everyone.

Eventually it was too much for most people. Most of his family shunned him and no longer invited him to family gatherings, little occasions—like Christmas.

Friends gave up on him. It's hard to continue to help and support someone who seems to be hurting themselves over and over again. Few friendships can endure that forever.

The truck would have to be rescued from impoundment. There would be overdue bills to pay, and later, tickets for leaving his vehicle too long somewhere would arrive in the mail.

He was often put out immediately by whoever his landlord or roommate was.

Penniless and homeless, he would go to the few remaining people in his life that would still talk to him and shame-faced, beg ten dollars here, fifty dollars there, enough to find a place to stay—a shelter, a couch or a cockroach-infested motel room. There was no dignity.

With stress, anxiety and shame weighing him down, he would put his life back together, go to daily AA meetings, find work as a contractor, repay each penny, try to put shaky relationships back together, get through isolation and loneliness and enormous guilt, work out to rebuild his physical strength, buy back a few belongings from the pawn shop.

He would continue to try to seek help, setting up an appointment with a psychiatrist that specialized in addiction or turning to a local center for mental health.

And then, in two to three months, he would do it all over again.

French-American cardiologist and former alcoholic, the late Dr. Olivier Ameisen was truly right when he wrote, "Addiction is a living nightmare in which you wake up *to* the horror, not *from* it.[22]

You know those people you walk past downtown? The ones lying on a hot air vent, covered in a piece of cardboard on a downtown street? I always wondered, 'what goes on in someone's life for them to end up there?'

But now I have a better idea of the answer to that. I always thought Randy was one binge away from becoming one of those people.

•••

I was told at Alanon meetings and by others not to help him.

They said, "He has to hit rock bottom before he will change. Practice 'tough love.'" I'd feel guilty for the $50 I'd lend him or for giving him a drive somewhere. I thought they were right, so for a long time I did nothing to help him–I wouldn't lift a finger–and I'd get angry at anyone who did.

But every time I saw this cycle, I'd wonder, if he hasn't hit this so-called 'rock bottom' yet, what can rock bottom *possibly* look like?

Because every three months I saw him go through a hell that would knock most human beings off their feet and put them in a psychiatric ward for a month.

It was unbelievable to see what he endured. It was unbelievable to see him get back on his feet again and again.

•••

He might have been an addict, but he had a big heart, and he never stopped being a human being who hurt–a lot.

I never saw Randy cry about his own material losses. But I did see this big guy bawl his eyes out like a child in pain over the hurt he had caused people he cared for over and over again.

He would say, "I am such a F—ing idiot! I'm such a stupid F-up!"

And he always defended to me the people who treated him badly. He knew how much his alcoholism had hurt them too and was somehow able to forgive them.

As the alcohol left his system after a binge sometimes I'd help him write a 'to do' list.

He was so overwhelmed by the enormity and anxiety of everything he had to fix that the list usually had no more than four tasks on it.

I found an old one the other day while I was cleaning up. It had tasks like, 'eat soup', and 'find truck' written on it.

As anyone would be, he would be overwhelmed by the enormity and anxiety of everything he had to fix.

•••

In between binges, my friend was a different person. At first he was relieved and happy to be sober and in control again. It was like he had gotten something out of his system and could think straight again.

He rebuilt his life each and every time.

When he was sober he was a dedicated and popular member of AA. Shamefaced, after a binge he'd walk back into a meeting and get his first chip all over again. After he died I found lots of those chips. They were a little reminder of something that had offered so much hope.

He read the AA big book, wrote in a journal, practiced the steps, worked with a sponsor, prayed, made amends, and attended meetings nearly every day.

AA was comforting to him. And he loved a lot of the people there (and they loved him). Without the community he had in AA maybe he would not have lasted as long as he did.

But it had no effect whatsoever when it came to helping him control alcoholism.

And inevitably, after a few months, that straight thinking would disintegrate.

•••

I'd been doing some research, so one day Randy and I watched Claudia Christian's amazing documentary 'One Little Pill'.

It was utterly enthralling.

This pill, naltrexone–why hadn't we heard about it? Where could we get some? Would it work? We were so hopeful.

There are some very vivid scenes of drinking in that documentary, and I believe Randy was very strongly triggered by the alcohol cues in those scenes.

The next morning he went to his family doctor and convinced his reticent doctor to give him a prescription for naltrexone. Then he went to the liquor store. He didn't bother to stop at the pharmacy in between.

I picked him up at his apartment and despite the fact that he was already drunk, I marched him off to the pharmacy where we handed in the prescription. I was used to double-takes when I was with him—the sober girl, and the drunk guy.

They didn't have naltrexone—barely knew of it. We waited in the drugstore as they called around to other pharmacies for us and finally located 30 pills at one of them.

Thirty pills was the entire supply of naltrexone in a city of several hundred thousand people. Either there was a huge, unprecedented run on naltrexone or not too many doctors were prescribing it. I hope nobody else needed them. Another car ride, and three hundred uninsured dollars later, we had the pills and he took one.

Naltrexone stopped the binge in its tracks.

He went to work the next day.

That was unheard of.

The next night he came over with a bottle of wine.

He took a pill, and took a drink of wine.

The rest of the bottle sat there on the counter, untouched for the rest of the evening. I still have a photograph of it. It was unbelievable.

The naltrexone seemed to work.

There is research that shows that those with the most severe alcoholism (as Randy clearly had) are also the ones who may have the most difficulty in compliance with naltrexone—or in other words, they are likely to stop taking it when they are supposed to.

And that's what happened with Randy—he stopped taking it.

In a way it was devastating. Here was something that worked for him, but also didn't work for him. Hope came and hope went.

Someone asked me—'why did he stop taking it? That was so stupid!'

I said he stopped for the same reason he drank—because there was a very sick brain inside his head making all of the decisions. There was not enough healthy brain left to just keep taking that damn one little pill.

One of my biggest regrets is that I didn't take the next step with him.

I could have driven him across the border to receive the monthly naltrexone injection. Things might have been very different for him.

But I didn't.

•••

Randy could tell his AA sponsor any transgression he had ever made. As is customary in AA, they worked through many of his most painful moments in life together.

But he only once brought medication up with his sponsor, and the reaction he received taught him never to bring it up again.

I brought it up with his sponsor too—someone I thought was intelligent, logical and well-reasoned. The sponsor sent me a link to an article that said medication was a waste of time and a crutch. I also got the very clear message not to bring it up again.

It was my first experience bringing the idea of medication to an AA member, other than Randy, and it taught me that AA and medication didn't mix.

•••

After the naltrexone experience, Randy jumped through a lot of hoops to get into a well-respected public program that indicated they treated alcoholics with, among other things, medication.

I'd read a lot more about other medications and we were hopeful that he'd find something that could help him manage the disease.

We went back and forth, an hour drive each way, several times.

There was an initial interview meeting, then another day spent watching a presentation made by a social worker, and then a few months of waiting for an appointment with the addictions specialist. Again – this experience of reaching out for help and finding that actually getting it was very difficult.

Finally, he drove into the city again for the doctor's appointment.

I talked to him after the appointment. I was hopeful that he had finally met an enlightened doctor—one with experience and knowledge in medical treatment of alcoholism.

But that wasn't the case.

He said the doctor was not very enthusiastic about medication. The 'medical' advice he'd received?

Keep going to AA.

•••

When he binged, Randy almost always drove drunk.

And he wasn't alone in this—attend enough AA meetings and you'll find it's common practice for alcoholics. (And while it seems to me that combatting alcoholism should be high on the radar for organizations that advocate against drunk driving, inquiries to a few of the major ones in North America told me it isn't).

The second last time I saw my friend binge, he had not eaten for at least a week, had been drinking 40 ouncers of vodka day and night for two weeks, had been seen stumbling around half naked in the parking lot of a seedy motel, was still driving around in his truck to pick up liquor, was vomiting up dark liquid and had several severe bruises and gashes on his body from falls.

I found him this way after the police called me to report that he'd been in a car accident and left the scene. (They didn't know he'd been drinking). He was in a motel right next to the accident location.

You don't need to be a doctor to predict that if this is what your life looks like, it won't be long before you are in a drawer at the morgue.

This was bad, but it wasn't unusual. And so, long before this particular binge, I had become convinced that he would be dead within 5 years.

I told a member of his family this and suggested that she should try to enjoy him while he was still around.

He was fun to be around when he was sober, and when he was drinking he was never mean–just the opposite–sometimes he was grumpy and stubborn, but usually he was quite introspective, honest and gentle.

I guess she heard me because after that conversation he was invited to their house for dinner a few times.

•••

Einstein says the definition of insanity is doing the same thing over and over, and expecting different results.

But that's what we did. He'd relapse, we—his friends and family— would get mad at him. He'd grovel. Holier than thou, we'd deign to let him back into our 'good graces' saying, "this is the last time!" Then the whole thing would happen all over again.

If Randy was relapsing on a regular, consistent basis, why were we always so disappointed and angry with him each time? What good did it really do? In retrospect, it was just very harmful. I started to take a new approach.

Later I thought of it as a kind of palliative care.

If a 'palliative care' approach existed for severe addicts, instead of this one where we just wait for rock bottom, and make life no easier for the alcoholic, then maybe Randy's last few years on this earth could have been not so hellish. Maybe he would still be here.

It took me a lot of time–and seeing the cycle over and over again to come to this perspective.

I know many people would call some of my behavior 'enabling'–I would once have done the same. But eventually I came to the conclusion that if 'tough love' was going to save Randy it would have worked already.

When he drank before, I was sometimes unkind. I would stay away from him until he stopped. If he showed up at the house I wouldn't let him in. But given the perspective that things weren't going to change for Randy, I started to behave differently.

For example, when he was in the middle of a binge, I knew he was lonely and trapped in a basement or dingy motel, so I'd take him with me to a dog park.

I got more than a few funny looks from people, but I didn't care. He was not a threat to anyone, and he loved the dogs.

I'd take him to the beach for an hour for fresh air and some company and food. We'd sit on a rock and when he started getting antsy for more alcohol I'd take him back.

If he stopped by the house, instead of keeping him locked out as I would have before, I let him in for a while.

And if he wanted to go to detox, I'd take him.

When I wrote this part of the book, Randy was still alive. I knew he would die, but not so soon.

And during that time when he was alive I wrote this, "I sometimes think forward to the day when I am at his funeral and, as sad as I know it will be, I don't want to have any regrets about making his life worse than it already was. I want to know that he knew I saw him as a good human who deserved dignity, and showed him love and kindness."

The best advice I can give to anyone, when it comes to how you interact with someone you love, whether they are an addict or not, is to think about how you will feel at their funeral.

I'm no saint. I didn't always treat him well—I was angry at him. I did a lot of things wrong. But I'm thankful that mostly I was kind to him, and I was particularly kind after I realized he wasn't going to get better. And I'm so glad of that.

And because of this, while I do feel regret and guilt at his death, I feel far less, I know, than others.

•••

I had not seen him for a while, but I heard later that over the summer of 2015 Randy was doing really well—on the outside anyways.

He had friends over for a barbecue and played guitar out in his garden for them.

He walked his puppy around his townhouse complex and made friends with new neighbors.

He was spending time with his son—the person on this earth he loved the most–who was working with him over the summer.

He was working hard–something he loved to do, making money in his roofing company, paying off debts, working out, dating.

He was spending time with people in his family that would still include him in their lives and as usual, he kept on trying to mend fences, repairing relationships with friends and family that shunned him. He reunited with his childhood best friend. They planned to play hockey together again in the fall. He looked tanned and fit.

But on May 21 he texted me saying he was "struggling hard." We talked but there was not much I could do.

If his life was a train wreck, then this was the start of the final moments of that wreck–when things start happening in slow motion and you can see it happening in front of you, but you can't stop it.

A week later he gave away his dog.

Around June 8 he started to drink again.

A few more weeks of hard drinking, and on June 24 he told me he wanted to kill himself. He said he no longer wanted to hurt the people that loved him. He didn't see how he could move on with his life–be in a relationship with anyone ever again–when he could never seem to stay sober. He didn't want to make his mom cry anymore. He was out of hope.

I took him to detox the next day. All the way there he kept asking me to turn around and telling me he just wanted to kill himself and I kept telling him it would be okay, to reconsider. (It wasn't the first time I'd heard this from him during a relapse).

I got him into the detox, but a few hours later he checked himself out.

The detox called the police. They had a duty to do so because he was suicidal. That's another pattern for people with addiction that is very common. Eventually an addict that the medical system has failed enters the criminal justice system–so that system can fail him too.

Over the next few weeks he continued to drink. He texted and called friends and family and said goodbye.

He said he loved them and told them he was going to die soon. Some responded. Others didn't. Some called the police. Others ignored him.

I could have been there more for him, but I'd made a decision to live my own life. That feels bad enough, so I can't imagine how the people who loved him that completely ignored him feel now, in retrospect.

But at the time, I guess they'd already made a decision to get off the train too. Ultimately, we all have one life to live. We have to live it for ourselves. Sometimes being around someone as sick as Randy is so destructive, we just have to let them go.

There was a period of three days in a psych ward where he was forced to stop drinking (nobody visited). I drove him home and he started back up again.

Friends called the police, worried about him. The police visited him several times. He was always drinking when they called on him—he was never taken seriously.

But show me an alcoholic who has ever committed suicide when he or she was sober.

On July 12 Randy was arrested for drunk driving. That was probably the last straw—more than he could bear.

On July 22 Randy went to the police station for finger printing for the drunk driving charge.

I believe that sometime the next day, July 23, 2015 he hung himself.

He got off the train too.

No more smiling, no more laughing, no more guitar playing, no more drinking, no more Randy.

•••

Randy's sponsor talked about Randy's 'allergy to alcohol' at his funeral.

Hearing this stupid notion (which I'd heard many times before from AA members and read in the AA Big Book), made me cringe.

The last thing I wanted Randy's funeral to serve as was a platform to continue to further the antiquated, incorrect notions about this disease.

Alcoholism is no more an allergy than any mental or physical illness is. If it were, I would have just about stabbed him to death with my daughter's EpiPen years ago.

I notified Randy's psychiatrist a few weeks after his death that Randy had taken his life.

It's not a shameful secret that he killed himself, at least, I won't let it be. It's a fact of this untreated disease.

And it was his way—a way I know took enormous courage—the only way he knew—for Randy to stop the devastation his disease left in his wake.

His psychiatrist—an addiction specialist—a doctor with medical training—wrote me, "thank you for letting me know. I had no idea. Addiction is a horrible condition... The use of that stuff destroys the soul."

I know he had cared about Randy. But the words he used stuck with me. His soul? Really?

It's no wonder that in the days before his death Randy wrote to me and told me he felt like a monster.

I replied to the shrink: "It definitely destroyed parts of his brain, but his soul was still beautiful." In retrospect—it was mean-spirited of me. I was lashing out.

But again—these beliefs and phrases—they aren't right. No doctor would say that Alzheimer's had destroyed someone's 'soul', or that schizophrenia had destroyed a 'soul'.

I can't think of anyone—perhaps other than a murderer or pedophile—who would deserve that description.

An 'allergy' to alcohol? An illness that destroys 'the soul'?

It is the subtleties of language and behavior like these that are the shadows of the massive, looming illogic with which we treat this illness.

Despite the wealth of medical knowledge we have that addiction is an illness of the brain, despite the medical treatments that exist, his sponsor thought he had an allergy and his doctor thought he needed to fix his soul.

No wonder Randy never got better. He never really had a chance.

YOUR STORY

But you do have a chance.

Whether you are just starting to realize you are developing dependence, or you already know you have a serious problem with alcoholism, today you have a far better chance than Randy ever had.

He didn't have this book.

You do.

These medications exist. And now all of this information is here, in one place, for you.

It's up to you now.

My hope for you is that you don't become another sad story.

I couldn't save Randy. But my hope is that this book might help save someone else. Maybe you.

I wish you all the best, and I hope you can do what you need to do to live the beautiful and amazing life you were meant to live.

I hope you can find a way to be happy, joyous, and free.

Namaste.

08 | RESOURCES

APRESCRIPTIONFORALCOHOLICS.COM

If you would like additional information on this topic, I encourage you to visit the book website, located at APrescriptionForAlcoholics.com.

There you will find:

- At least one free book excerpt that you can share with others.

- A list of recommended reading which includes some of the best and most informative research articles, reports, popular press articles, and books.

You'll also find links to:

- Key research, reports, and publications mentioned in this book

- Forums and support groups

- Links to online pharmacies

The site will be updated and expanded over time, so please join the mailing list for updates.

SPREAD THE WORD

If this book has made a difference to you, please consider helping to spread the word.

You can do this by:

- Sharing the free chapter found on the website with a friend (www.APrescriptionforAlcoholics.com)

- Passing the book on to someone you know.

- Donating a few copies to a library, school, doctor's office or recovery program.

- Posting about the book on social media.

BIBLIOGRAPHY

The bibliography is also available at the book website (APrescriptionforAlcoholics.com). The site will be updated in the future to include a searchable database of links to bibliography publications. Some printable publications are already available on the website.

If you would like to be updated when the full database is available, sign-up for the newsletter at the book website.

1.   Heilig M, Egli M. Pharmacological treatment of alcohol dependence: Target symptoms and target mechanisms. *Pharmacol Ther.* 2006;111(3):855-876. doi:10.1016/j.pharmthera.2006.02.001.
2.   Batki SL, Pennington DL. Toward personalized medicine in the pharmacotherapy of alcohol use disorder: Targeting patient genes and patient goals. *Am J Psychiatry.* 2014;171(4):391-394. doi:10.1176/appi.ajp.2014.14010061.
3.   Addiction Medicine: Closing the Gap Between Science & Practice | CASAColumbia. http://www.casacolumbia.org/addiction-research/reports/addiction-medicine. Accessed November 11, 2015.
4.   Heilig M. The Thirteenth Step Addiction in the Age of Brain Science. 2015.
5.   Ferri M, Amato L, Davoli M. Alcoholics Anonymous and other 12-step programmes for alcohol dependence. *Cochrane Database Syst Rev.* 2006;3(3):CD005032. doi:10.1002/14651858.CD005032.pub2.
6.   White N. Alcoholics Anonymous has a terrible success rate, addiction expert finds. *Tor Star.* 2014:2-5. http://www.thestar.com/life/2014/03/28/alcoholics_anonymous_has_a_terrible_success_rate_addiction_expert_finds.html.

7.   Author Unknown. Medication for the Treatment of Alcohol Use Disorder: A Brief Guide. *NIAAA*. 2013. http://store.samhsa.gov/shin/content/SMA15-4907/SMA15-4907.pdf.

8.   Kraft S. WHO Study: Alcohol Is International Number One Killer, AIDS Second. *MedicalNewsToday.com*. 2011. http://www.medicalnewstoday.com/articles/216328.php. Accessed April 30, 2015.

9.   World Health Organisation. Global status report on alcohol and health 2014. 2014:1-392. http://www.who.int/substance_abuse/publications/global_alcohol_report/msbgsruprofiles.pdf.

10.   Bradley K, Kivlahan D. Medications for alcohol use disorder--reply. *JAMA*. 2014;312(13):1352. doi:10.1001/jama.2014.10167.

11.   Dealing With Addiction: Why The 20th Century Was Wrong: Peter Ferentzy: 9781105004100: Amazon.com: Books. http://www.amazon.com/Dealing-With-Addiction-Century-Wrong/dp/1105004104. Accessed October 27, 2015.

12.   Merchant B. Less Than 1% of Oil-Soaked Birds Survive : TreeHugger. *TreeHugger*. 2010. http://www.treehugger.com/natural-sciences/less-than-1-of-oil-soaked-birds-survive.html. Accessed June 8, 2015.

13.   A Look At My Book. 2011. http://www.peterferentzy.com/Excerpt--A-Peek-Inside.html. Accessed October 21, 2015.

14.   Anahad O. Drugs to Aid Alcoholics See Little Use, Study Finds. *New York Times*. 2014:2014-2016. http://nyti.ms/1sqM915.

15.   Glaser G. The Irrationality of Alcoholics Anonymous. *Atl*. 2015. http://www.theatlantic.com/features/archive/2015/03/the-irrationality-of-alcoholics-anonymous/386255/. Accessed April 28, 2015.

16.   Batten L. Science and Technology Select Committee Inquiry on alcohol guidelines. Royal College of Physicians' Written Evidence. 2011;(September):1-12. doi:10.1111/j.1750-3841.2007.00606.x.

17.   Nutt D. Presentation: Alcohol Dependence: a Treatable

Brain Disease with Serious Health Consequences. In: ; 2014. ttp://progressinmind.elsevierresource.com/videos/lectures /burden-terms-increasing-mortality-rates.

18. Nutt D. Alcohol dependence : a treatable brain disease with serious health consequences. *Present ECNP*. 2014.

19. MADD - Drunk Driving Statistics. http://www.madd.org/drunk-driving/about/drunk-driving-statistics.html. Accessed September 3, 2015.

20. Unknown A. Children of Alcoholics. *Am Acad Child Adolesc Soc.* 2011;17(17):11-13. http://www.aacap.org/AACAP/Families_and_Youth/Fact s_for_Families/Facts_for_Families_Pages/Children_Of_Al coholics_17.aspx. Accessed April 30, 2015.

21. Kendall RE. Alcohol and suicide. *Subst Alcohol Actions Misuse.* 1983;4(2-3):121-127. http://www.ncbi.nlm.nih.gov/pubmed/6648755. Accessed April 30, 2015.

22. Ameisen O. The End of My Addiction. 2008. http://us.macmillan.com/theendofmyaddiction/olivieramei sen. Accessed May 18, 2015.

23. Measuring America's drinking habit is tricky – here's how to do it - The Washington Post. http://www.washingtonpost.com/news/wonkblog/wp/20 14/10/03/measuring-americas-drinking-habit-is-tricky-heres-how-to-do-it/. Accessed October 8, 2015.

24. Hazelden Introduces Antiaddiction Medications into Recovery for First Time | TIME.com. http://healthland.time.com/2012/11/05/hazelden-introduces-antiaddiction-medications-in-recovery-for-first-time/. Accessed November 2, 2015.

25. Release P. Lundbeck Introduces Selincro As the First and Only Medicine for the Reduction of Alcohol. *Eur Pharm Rev.* 2013:2-4.

26. Une recommandation temporaire d'utilisation (RTU) est accordée pour le baclofène - Point d'information - ANSM : Agence nationale de sécurité du médicament et des produits de santé. http://www.ansm.sante.fr/S-informer/Points-d-information-Points-d-information/Une-recommandation-temporaire-d-utilisation-RTU-est-

accordee-pour-le-baclofene-Point-d-information. Accessed November 11, 2015.

27. Michael Botticelli Sworn in as Deputy Director of the Office of National Drug Control Policy | whitehouse.gov. https://www.whitehouse.gov/ondcp/news-releases-remarks/botticelli-sworn-in-as-deputy-director-of-ondcp. Accessed October 30, 2015.

28. Obama Tells Outdated Opioid Treatment Industry It's Time To Change. http://www.huffingtonpost.com/entry/obama-opioid-addiction-treatment_5627b3d6e4b0bce347034174. Accessed October 29, 2015.

29. Alkermes PLC > Investor Relations > Press Release. http://phx.corporate-ir.net/phoenix.zhtml?c=92211&p=irol-newsArticle&ID=2072722. Accessed October 22, 2015.

30. Video & Transcript: President Obama Speech in Charleston, West Virginia on Prescription Drug Abuse and Heroin Addiction, Oct. 21, 2015 | Shallow Nation. http://www.shallownation.com/2015/10/21/video-president-obama-speech-in-charleston-west-virginia-on-prescription-drug-abuse-and-heroin-addiction-oct-21-2015/. Accessed October 29, 2015.

31. Addiction Resources | The Business of Recovery. http://www.thebusinessofrecovery.com/addiction-resources---the-business-of-recovery.html. Accessed October 9, 2015.

32. Del Re a C, Gordon AJ, Lembke A, Harris AHS. Prescription of topiramate to treat alcohol use disorders in the Veterans Health Administration. *Addict Sci Clin Pract.* 2013;8(1):12. doi:10.1186/1940-0640-8-12.

33. theNNT. http://www.thennt.com/. Accessed November 26, 2015.

34. Kalk NJ, Lingford-Hughes AR. The clinical pharmacology of acamprosate. *Br J Clin Pharmacol.* 2012;77(2):315-323. doi:10.1111/bcp.12070.

35. Addolorato G, Leggio L, Ferrulli A, et al. Effectiveness and safety of baclofen for maintenance of alcohol abstinence in alcohol-dependent patients with liver cirrhosis: randomised, double-blind controlled study. *Lancet.* 2007;370(9603):1915-

1922. doi:10.1016/S0140-6736(07)61814-5.

36. Fletcher DK. New Treatments for Alcohol Related Problems. *Presentation*. 2014.

37. Mason BJ, Quello S, Goodell V, Shadan F, Kyle M, Begovic A. Gabapentin treatment for alcohol dependence a randomized clinical trial. *JAMA Intern Med*. 2014;174(1):70-77. doi:10.1001/jamainternmed.2013.11950.

38. Spanagel R, Vengeliene V, Jandeleit B, et al. Acamprosate produces its anti-relapse effects via calcium. *Neuropsychopharmacology*. 2013;39(4):783-791. doi:10.1038/npp.2013.264.

39. Higuchi S. Efficacy of Acamprosate for the Treatment of Alcohol Dependence Long After Recovery From Withdrawal Syndrome. *J Clin Psychiatry*. 2015;(February):181-188. doi:10.4088/JCP.13m08940.

40. Mason BJ, Lehert P. Acamprosate for Alcohol Dependence: A Sex-Specific Meta-Analysis Based on Individual Patient Data. *Alcohol Clin Exp Res*. 2012;36(3):497-508. doi:10.1111/j.1530-0277.2011.01616.x.

41. Soyka M, Kranzler HR, Berglund M, et al. World Federation of Societies of Biological Psychiatry (WFSBP) Guidelines for Biological Treatment of Substance Use and Related Disorders, Part 1: Alcoholism. *world J Biol psychiatry*. 2008;9(1):6-23. doi:10.1080/15622970801896390.

42. Rosack J. Once-Promising Alcoholism Drug Runs Into FDA Roadblock. *Psychiatr News*. 2014. http://psychnews.psychiatryonline.org/doi/full/10.1176/p n.37.17.0024a. Accessed May 7, 2015.

43. Agabio R, Colombo G. GABAB receptor ligands for the treatment of alcohol use disorder: preclinical and clinical evidence. *Front Neurosci*. 2014;8:140. doi:10.3389/fnins.2014.00140.

44. De Beaurepaire R. Suppression of alcohol dependence using baclofen: A 2-year observational study of 100 patients. *Front Psychiatry*. 2012;3(DEC):1-7. doi:10.3389/fpsyt.2012.00103.

45. Johnson B a, Ait-Daoud N. Topiramate in the new generation of drugs: efficacy in the treatment of alcoholic patients. *Curr Pharm Des*. 2010;16(19):2103-2112. doi:10.2174/138161210791516404.

46.   Leavitt SB. Evidence for the Efficacy of Naltrexone in the Treatment of Alcohol Dependence (Alcoholism). *Addict Treat Forum*. 2002.

47.   Haass-Koffler CL, Leggio L, Kenna G a. Pharmacological Approaches to Reducing Craving in Patients with Alcohol Use Disorders. *CNS Drugs*. 2014;28(4):1-18. doi:10.1007/s40263-014-0149-3.

48.   Harris AHS, Bowe T, Del Re AC, et al. Extended Release Naltrexone for Alcohol Use Disorders: Quasi-Experimental Effects on Mortality and Subsequent Detoxification Episodes. *Alcohol Clin Exp Res*. 2015;39(1):79-83. doi:10.1111/acer.12597.

49.   Greutman MD, Gales MA, Gales BJ, Greutman MD, Gales BJ. Gabapentin in Alcohol Dependence. *J Pharm Technol*. 2015:8755122515575543. doi:10.1177/8755122515575543.

50.   Unknown A. Clinical Trial Indicates Gabapentin Is Safe and Effective for Treating Alcohol Dependence. *Scripps.edu*. 2013. http://www.scripps.edu/newsandviews/e_20131111/mason.html. Accessed May 3, 2015.

51.   ADial: Pharmacotherapeutics for dependence-related diseases. http://www.adialpharma.com/products/. Accessed October 22, 2015.

52.   Litten RZ, Bradley AM, Moss HB. Alcohol biomarkers in applied settings: Recent advances and future research opportunities. *Alcohol Clin Exp Res*. 2010;34(6):955-967. doi:10.1111/j.1530-0277.2010.01170.x.

53.   Author Unknown. The Corporate, Political and Scientific History of Naltrexone. *Low Dose Naltrexone*. 2015. http://www.lowdosenaltrexone.org/gazorpa/History.html.

54.   Together J, Field AE. Medication for Alcoholism : An Expanding Field. 2012.

55.   Alcohol dependency: burden in terms of stigmatization - Psychiatry. http://progressinmind.elsevierresource.com/videos/lectures/burden-terms-stigmatization. Accessed October 5, 2015.

56.   Clinical relevance of alcohol reduction | Progress in Mind: Focus on Alcohol Use Disorders Resource Centre. http://progressinmind.elsevierresource.com/videos/lectures/clinical-relevance-alcohol-reduction. Accessed October 5,

2015.
57. Fda. Novel New Drugs 2014. *Cent Drug Eval Res.* 2015;(January):0-18. doi:http://www.fda.gov/downloads/Drugs/Development ApprovalProcess/DrugInnovation/UCM430299.pdf.
58. What Addicts Need. http://www.newsweek.com/what-addicts-need-93767. Accessed October 23, 2015.
59. Pink Ribbons Inc. takes a close look at breast cancer fundraising | National Post. http://news.nationalpost.com/arts/the-women-behind-pink-ribbons-inc-hope-to-change-the-discourse-of-breast-cancer. Accessed October 20, 2015.
60. Eddy DM. The Origins of Evidence-Based Medicine. A Personal Perspective. *Virtual Mentor.* 2011;13(1):55-60. doi:10.1001/virtualmentor.2011.13.1.mhst1-1101.
61. Dodes L. The Sober Truth: Debunking the Bad Science Behind 12-Step Programs and the Rehab Industry. *Book.* 2014. http://www.amazon.com/The-Sober-Truth-Debunking-Programs/dp/0807033154. Accessed April 30, 2015.
62. Miller JC. 12-step treatment for alcohol and substance abuse revisted: Best available evidence suggests lack of effectiveness or harm. *Int J Ment Health Addict.* 2008;6(4):568-576. doi:10.1007/s11469-008-9146-4.
63. Letters 30. http://www.orange-papers.org/orange-letters30.html. Accessed October 29, 2015.
64. Dying To Be Free - The Huffington Post. http://projects.huffingtonpost.com/dying-to-be-free-heroin-treatment. Accessed October 30, 2015.
65. Donovan DM, Ingalsbe MH, Benbow J, Daley DC. 12-step interventions and mutual support programs for substance use disorders: an overview. *Soc Work Public Health.* 2013;28(3-4):313-332. doi:10.1080/19371918.2013.774663.
66. DuPont RL, McLellan a. T, White WL, Merlo LJ, Gold MS. Setting the standard for recovery: Physicians' Health Programs. *J Subst Abuse Treat.* 2009;36(2):159-171. doi:10.1016/j.jsat.2008.01.004.
67. Alcoholics Anonymous World Services. Three Talks to Medical Societies by Bill W., Co-Founder of Alcoholics Anonymous. *Alcohol Anon.* 1949:4-32.

68.   As Bill Sees It: The A.A. Way of Life-- Selected Writings of A.A.'s Co-Founder: Alcoholics Anonymous World Service, Bill W: 9780916856038: Books - Amazon.ca. http://www.amazon.ca/As-Bill-Sees-It-Co-Founder/dp/0916856038. Accessed September 28, 2015.

69.   Wilson B. A Communication to AAs Physicians - Vitamin B. *Unpublished*. 1965.

70.   Goodman C, Ahn R, Harwood R. Case Studies : LAAM , Naltrexone , Clozapine , and Nicorette. *Dep Heal Hum Serv*. 1997. http://aspe.hhs.gov/health/reports/cocaine/FINAL.htm.

71.   Ferentzy P, Turner NE. *The History of Problem Gambling: Temperance, Substance Abuse, Medicine, and Metaphors*. Springer Science & Business Media; 2013. https://books.google.com/books?id=gZlAAAAAQBAJ&pgis=1. Accessed September 3, 2015.

72.   *The Big Book of Alcoholics Anonymous*.

73.   Inside Addiction Treatment With Dr. Marvin Seppala | The Fix. https://www.thefix.com/content/inside-addiction-with-marvin-seppala. Accessed October 30, 2015.

74.   Founding Story |. http://www.compassion4addiction.org/about/founding-story/. Accessed October 27, 2015.

75.   Larimer ME, Palmer RS, Marlatt GA. Relapse prevention: An overview of Marlatt's Cognitive-Cehavioral Model. *Alcohol Res Heal*. 1999;23(2):151-160. doi:10.1186/1747-597X-6-17.

76.   Mignon SI. Physicians' Perceptions of Alcoholics. *Alcohol Treat Q*. 1996;14(4):33-45. doi:10.1300/J020V14N04_02.

77.   Ghfoduhg KDG, Dofrkrolvp W, Dq ZD V, Lq L. Disease theory of alcoholism.

78.   Nunes E V. Gabapentin: a new addition to the armamentarium for alcohol dependence? *JAMA Intern Med*. 2014;174(1):78-79. doi:10.1001/jamainternmed.2013.11973.

79.   Schomerus G, Lucht M, Holzinger A, Matschinger H, Carta MG, Angermeyer MC. The stigma of alcohol dependence compared with other mental disorders: A review of population studies. *Alcohol Alcohol*. 2011;46(2):105-112. doi:10.1093/alcalc/agq089.

80.   Juman RM. The Deadly Stigma of Addiction. *Fix*. 2012:1-

30.
81. "My hope that women will not be afraid": Classic Actresses who had Breast Cancer | Comet Over Hollywood on WordPress.com. http://cometoverhollywood.com/2015/10/23/my-hope-that-women-will-not-be-afraid-classic-actresses-who-had-breast-cancer/. Accessed October 28, 2015.
82. Pescosolido BA, Martin JK, Long JS, Medina TR, Phelan JC, Link BG. "A disease like any other"? A decade of change in public reactions to schizophrenia, depression, and alcohol dependence. *Am J Psychiatry*. 2010;167(11):1321-1330. doi:10.1176/appi.ajp.2010.09121743.
83. Inside The $35 Billion Addiction Treatment Industry - Forbes. http://www.forbes.com/sites/danmunro/2015/04/27/inside-the-35-billion-addiction-treatment-industry/. Accessed October 21, 2015.
84. Targeting Addiction | The University of Virginia Magazine. http://uvamagazine.org/articles/targeting_addiction/. Accessed October 23, 2015.
85. Butler D. Translational research: crossing the valley of death. *Nature*. 2008;453(7197):840-842. doi:10.1038/453840a.
86. Uxj DQG, Dqg G, Wkdw F, et al. List of off-label promotion pharmaceutical settlements. 2005.
87. Mason BJ, Quello S, Goodell V, Shadan F, Kyle M, Begovic A. Gabapentin treatment for alcohol dependence a randomized clinical trial. *JAMA Intern Med*. 2014;174(1):70-77. http://www.embase.com/search/results?subaction=viewrecord&from=export&id=L372116393\nhttp://dx.doi.org/10.1001/jamainternmed.2013.11950\nhttp://elvis.ubvu.vu.nl:9003/vulink?sid=EMBASE&issn=21686106&id=doi:10.1001/jamainternmed.2013.11950&atitle=Gabapent.
88. Release C, Markets I. Major restructuring initiative announced and 2015 guidance revised - Lundbeck. 2015;(56759913):1-24.
89. Big pharma pulling back from mental health | CTV News. 2012. http://www.ctvnews.ca/health/health-headlines/big-pharma-pulling-back-from-mental-health-drug-research-

studies-1.1015154. Accessed October 22, 2015.

90. The great neuro-pipeline "brain drain" (and why Big Pharma hasn't given up on CNS disorders). http://www.ddw-online.com/therapeutics/p216813-the-great-neuro-pipeline-brain-drain-(and-why-big-pharma-hasn-t-given-up-on-cns-disorders)-fall-13.html. Accessed October 23, 2015.

91. Kaitin KI, Milne CP. A Dearth of New Meds. *Sci Am.* 2011;305(2):16-16. doi:10.1038/scientificamerican0811-16.

92. RB spin-out Indivior says addiction pipeline will deliver - News - pharmaphorum. http://www.pharmaphorum.com/news/rb-spin-out-indivior-says-addiction-pipeline-will-deliver. Accessed June 9, 2015.

93. Unknown A. Reckitt Benckiser Pharmaceuticals and XenoPort Enter Into Global Licensing Agreement for Arbaclofen Placarbil (NASDAQ:XNPT). *Website.* 2013. http://investor.xenoport.com/releasedetail.cfm?ReleaseID =848226. Accessed June 4, 2015.

94. Indivior understands a patient's journey with addiction. http://indivior.com/diseases-of-addiction/the-patient-journey/. Accessed October 22, 2015.

95. Turncliff R, DiPetrillo L, Silverman B, Ehrich E. Single- and multiple-dose pharmacokinetics of samidorphan, a novel opioid antagonist, in healthy volunteers. *Clin Ther.* 2015;37(2):338-348. doi:10.1016/j.clinthera.2014.10.001.

96. Neuroscience Drug Discovery Research | AstraZeneca. http://openinnovation.astrazeneca.com/az-rd-focus-areas/neuroscience/. Accessed October 22, 2015.

97. ADial Pharmaceuticals Announces Publication of Study on AD04 for the Treatment of Patients With Alcohol Use Disorder | Reuters. http://www.reuters.com/article/2013/08/12/idUSnGNX6 Pzsps+1d0+GNW20130812. Accessed October 16, 2015.

98. Addex Therapeutics : Addex' ADX71441 Demonstrates Robust Efficacy in Multiple Preclinical Models of Alcohol Use Disorder. http://www.addextherapeutics.com/investors/press-releases/news-details/article/addex-adx71441-demonstrates-robust-efficacy-in-multiple-preclinical-

models-of-alcohol-use-disorde/. Accessed October 22, 2015.

99. Kroll D. XenoPort And NIAAA To Test Alcoholism Treatment. *Forbes.* 2014. http://www.forbes.com/sites/davidkroll/2014/09/10/xen oport-and-niaaa-to-test-alcoholism-treatment/. Accessed June 9, 2015.

100. Welcome to XenoPort. http://www.xenoport.com/. Accessed October 22, 2015.

101. AstraZeneca Working with Eolas Therapeutics on Anti-Addiction Drug | Xconomy. http://www.xconomy.com/san-diego/2015/06/30/astrazeneca-working-with-eolas-therapeutics-on-anti-addiction-drug/. Accessed October 22, 2015.

102. Heptares - Pipeline. http://www.heptares.com/pipeline/. Accessed October 22, 2015.

103. Unknown A. SMO. *http://www.da-pharma.fr/*. 2015.

104. Ferraro L, Loche A, Beggiato S, et al. The new compound GET73, N-[(4-trifluoromethyl)benzyl]4-methoxybutyramide, Regulates hippocampal Aminoacidergic transmission possibly via an allosteric modulation of mGlu5 receptor. Behavioural evidence of its "anti-alcohol" and anxiolytic properties. *Curr Med Chem.* 2013;20(27):3339-3357. http://www.ncbi.nlm.nih.gov/pubmed/23862615. Accessed July 9, 2015.

105. A Conversation With Michael Botticelli, The New Director Of National Drug Control Policy - The Diane Rehm Show. http://thedianerehmshow.org/shows/2015-06-11/a-conversation-with-michael-botticelli-the-new-white-house-drug-czar. Accessed October 29, 2015.

106. SAMHSA bans drug court grantees from ordering participants off MAT. http://www.alcoholismdrugabuseweekly.com/m-article-detail/samhsa-bans-drug-court-grantees-from-ordering-participants-off-mat.aspx. Accessed October 29, 2015.

107. Linchpin: Are You Indispensable?: Seth Godin: 8601400965627: Amazon.com: Books. http://www.amazon.com/Linchpin-Are-Indispensable-

Seth-Godin/dp/1591844096. Accessed October 27, 2015.

108. Thomas PE. Suppression of alcohol dependence using high-dose baclofen: A self-case report. *Prog Neurol Psychiatry*. 2012;16(1):30-31. doi:10.1002/pnp.226.

109. "John" David Sinclair - Times West Virginian: Obituaries. http://www.timeswv.com/obituaries/john-david-sinclair/article_eb3ee6be-f39c-11e4-8145-4f42ac610bd0.html. Accessed December 7, 2015.

110. Unknown A. Lundbeck Nalmefene Patent Overview. *Eur Pat Off.* 2015.

111. Unknown A. US2014005216A1 - nalmefene lundbeck patent jan 2014.pdf. *Pat Appl.* 2014.

112. Sinclair JD. Method for treating alcoholism with nalmefene - Patent. *United States Pat Database*. 1992:1-7.

113. Sinclair JD. US Patent for Naltrexone. *United States Pat Database*. 1989:1-8.

114. Babylon Confidential: A Memoir of Love, Sex, and Addiction: Claudia Christian, Morgan Grant Buchanan: 9781937856069: Amazon.com: Books. http://www.amazon.com/Babylon-Confidential-Memoir-Love-Addiction/dp/1937856062. Accessed December 7, 2015.

115. Glaser G. Her Best-Kept Secret: Why Women Drink-And How They Can Regain Control. *Book.* 2014. http://www.amazon.com/Her-Best-Kept-Secret-Drink-And-Control/dp/1439184380. Accessed April 30, 2015.

116. Article R, Schuckit MA. Recognition and Management of Withdrawal Delirium (Delirium Tremens). *N Engl J Med.* 2014;371(22):2109-2113. doi:10.1056/NEJMra1407298.

Made in the USA
Middletown, DE
30 September 2024

61741085R00116